Homosexuality
&
The Music Ministry

By

Allen Wicks

authorHOUSE™

1663 LIBERTY DRIVE, SUITE 200
BLOOMINGTON, INDIANA 47403
(800) 839-8640
WWW.AUTHORHOUSE.COM

First published by AuthorHouse 04/06/05

ISBN: 1-4184-8217-X (sc)

Printed in the United States of America
Bloomington, Indiana

This book is printed on acid-free paper.

Book Cover Design & Concept
Larry Rodgers c/o Forword Graphics
email: ForwordRecords@hotmail.com

Table of Contents

Foreword

This book is a "must read" for all Pastors, ministry leaders, and all concerned with music in our churches. In a day that we are swept away by music and lyrics. God has sent a word that brings the church and its music world to a screeching halt. The church world has been at ease in Zion because we are carried away with music and the voices.

Minister Allen Wicks clearly writes that the lifestyle is just as important as the song and music being rendered. This book gives the church a non-tolerant compassionate insight to addressing this great deception in the music ministry.

Ephesians 1:4 states, "According as he hath chosen us in Him before the foundation of the world, that we should be holy and without blame before Him in Love."

God is calling and has ordained for us to be holy and blameless. He is always reaching out to men to assist them in this calling. This book is reaching deep into the depths of deception with awesome instructions for those who are trapped to be set free to live the holy and blameless life our Savior is calling us to live.

Pastor Gary L. Pleasant
New Life Christian Church
Florissant, Missouri

Preface

Sacred music has been given to the church for edification, exhortation, and comfort. We as Christians must realize how music strengthens our faith and belief in God. God has invested the gift of music in the church to bring his presence and glory in the lives of his people. As we enter into the presence of God, He will reveal his nature and character to his people. The presence of God is necessary for the spiritual survival of the church. The anointing has been given to the church to destroy the yoke and works of the enemy that has people in bondage. The anointing and the presence of God must be protected in order for God's grace and mercy to remain in his church. As you read this book, pray that the spirit of wisdom, revelation, and knowledge be activated in you as you embrace this revelation from God.

This revelation from God was given to expose Satan's musical kingdom in the earth and in some churches. This revelation will also expose Satan's plan and purpose for the spirit of homosexuality in the world today.

> *Isaiah 10:37 – "And it shall come to pass in that day, that his burden shall be taken away from off thy shoulder, and his yoke from off thy neck, and the yoke shall be destroyed because of the anointing."*

"A Message To Satan"

Satan, it's high time that you be exposed to the body of Christ concerning your plan to try to stop or hinder God's plan of salvation for the human race. It's really amazing Satan that you still think within your mind that you will one day be like the "Most High God." In an effort to receive praise and worship like Jehovah God, you have intentionally perverted the minds and sexuality of many people in an attempt to keep them from being conformed to the image of God, which in turn will make them vessels that will offer you perverted praises and worship.

Down through the years many have fallen prey to your deception and schemes. Many have suffered from perverted lust and sexual orientation confusion. Satan, today is a new day because the revelation knowledge in this book will expose you for who and what you really are. Satan, you are a master liar and deceiver. It is written that because of the lack of knowledge, God's people are destroyed.

Well Satan, revelation knowledge has come from heaven to earth and it has the ability to open the eyes of those who are in spiritual darkness. It is only a matter of time before this knowledge spread throughout the earth. Once the church fully understands what you are trying to do, they will fight the kingdom of darkness as never before.

The church will awake out of its slumber and sleep with its passive attitude and realize that you have launched an attack on God's people whom he have ordained to carry his anointing and glory. Once we realize that there is a direct relationship between the Glory of God and the Ministry of Music, the church will begin to fight with a vengeance. So Satan, your days are numbered and your kingdom is now threatened by the revelation of God that's found in this book.

> II Cor 4:3-4, "But if our gospel be hid, it is hid to them that are lost. In whom the god of this world hath blinded the minds of them which believe not, lest the light of the glorious gospel of Christ, who is the image of God, should shine unto them."

GET BACK SATAN!

Minister Allen Wicks

Dedication

This book is dedicated to those who are suffering from sexual brokenness and from sexual orientation confusion. God feels your pain and sees your tears. Before the foundation of the world, God called and ordained us all to be holy and without blame before him. During this time God pre-ordained that we should all be sexually whole, and that is why God created Adam and Eve and placed within them an innate desire and attraction for one another. Keep in mind that your God given sexuality and sexual orientation is a gift from God. The sexual confusion you are experiencing is a work of the enemy. The Bible tells us that the enemy comes to steal, kill and destroy. 1 Cor. 14:33 informs us that God is not the author of confusion; For all of those individuals who have been struggling with deception and bondage, I want you to look up because your redemption draweth nigh.

Hebrews 4:15

For we have not a high priest which cannot be touched with the feelings of our infirmities: but was in all points tempted like as we are, yet without sin.

Introduction

The church of God has now entered into the new millennium and there are many demonic forces that will try to threaten the spiritual life of the church. One such issue is the problem of homosexuality and the music ministry. This has been a topic that many Christian leaders and individuals involved in the Gospel music industry cannot seem to adequately address nor deal with from a biblical perspective.

As the body of Christ progress further into the new millennium, it is imperative that we expose the spirit of homosexuality and how it is causing destruction in the lives of many singers, musicians, and others involved in the Arts. There have been countless numbers of musically inclined individuals within our churches who have died of AIDS or AIDS related illnesses. While the church is somewhat silent about this tragedy, the church needs to realize that the main goal of the spirit of homosexuality is to pervert the minds and sexuality of others, bringing them into sexual idolatry and bondage.

Many Christian churches and the pastoral leadership have opened the doors to this spirit, allowing it to infiltrate their congregations. What they fail to realize is that the spirit of homosexuality is a deceptive spirit that has the ability to lead others into ungodly musical worship that glorifies Satan and his musical kingdom.

It is high time that, the church, wake up out of its slumber and sleep and begin to wage war against this spirit that threatens God's plan for sexuality in the world and God's plan for music in the church. There have been many casualties in the lives of God's people because of ignorance on this topic, in addition to a lack of spiritual warfare by the church, to confront this issue. The church must take a stand and recognize that this spirit has the capability of gaining a stronghold in the church thus hindering the presence and the power of God from operating within our churches.

Chapter 1

Music, Sex, & Religion

The purpose of this chapter is to explore and see how music, sex and religion can have a devastating, negative affect on those who use them outside of God's ordained purpose. Whenever we use and apply principles of music, sex and religion outside of the God-given boundaries, we open up doors for Satan to come in and set up strong holds within our lives. These three portals have become the building blocks Satan is using to advance his purpose and kingdom in the earth. A portal can be defined as a door or gate to a particular person, place, or thing. There have been no other forces within the universe that have devastated human lives and changes the tides of history like that of music, sex and religion. These three portals within themselves, if used and experienced in the wrong way can cause cataclysmic

1

results in the lives of those who handle them without the fear of God in their lives.

Whenever we study history, we can see how Satan used music, sex, and religion to gain a foothold in the lives of millions of people. When we study historical facts about the Roman Empire we will find out that it was ungodly music, perverted sex, and religious idolatry that helped to bring down the Roman Empire. These three portals used together have the potential and capability to hinder or stop God's ordained purpose and destiny for his most prized creation, "mankind".

As you read this chapter further you will find out how the enemy has and is still using these portals in the universe to assist him in accomplishing his plan of destruction upon the earth. In John 10:10 the scriptures declare that the thief cometh not, but for to steal, and to kill and to destroy. Biblical history proves that Satan uses music, sex and religion as a strategic tool and weapon to destroy the moral fiber of a nation and eventually bring destruction to the lives of people. Ungodly music in the Old Testament helped to pervert a whole nation. Biblical scholars have discovered that ungodly music played a large role in the lifestyle of those who lived in Sodom and Gomorrah. We can see how King David was enticed into an adulterous sexual relationship with Bath-sheba that left a curse upon his entire household and family. Biblical history constantly reveals to us how the children of Israel forsook God and his commandments and began to worship false gods. Biblical history has proven over and over again that Satan uses a religious atmosphere and a religious system in order to promote a spirit of whoredom and idolatry eventually leading people into ungodly worship and temple prostitution.

Before we go further I want to clarify what I mean by a religious atmosphere and a religious system. A religious atmosphere can be defined as a religious environment that is conducive to the worship of a god other than the creator of the universe. Now a religious system can be described as an organized systematic belief system that is characterized by accepted rituals and ceremonial practices that are Christian and non-Christian in nature. The bible has proven that whenever mankind rejects and rebels against the ordinances and commandments of God that due to their disobedience, many people are led away by the spirit of whoredom into idol worship and sexual immorality.

Hosea 4:12-14 reads that "my people ask counsel at their stocks and their staff declareth unto them; for the spirit of whoredoms hath caused them to err, and they have gone a whoring from under their God. They sacrifice upon the tops of mountains, and burn incense upon the hills, under oaks and poplars, and elms, because the shadow there is good; therefore your daughters shall commit whoredom and your spouses shall commit adultery. I will not punish your daughters when they commit whoredom nor your spouses when they commit adultery; for they sacrifice with harlots; therefore the people that doth not understand shall fall."

These scriptures revealed to us what happened to Israel when they disobeyed God. This type of disobedience caused Israel to violate God's laws in its moral, social and religious aspects.

Now let us examine again what Hosea 4:12 stated, "For the spirit of whoredoms hath caused them to err."

3

The spirit of whoredom can be described as a demonic spirit of rebellion, that is anti-christ in nature, cloaked with a spirit of immorality, with the intent and purpose to lead people away from God into spiritual idolatry and sexual immorality.

The latter part of verse 12 states that the spirit of whoredom can cause people to err. To err in general means to violate an accepted moral standard. And in this context it addresses the word of God. To err also means to forsake a God-ordained mandate that can result in apostasy. One of the main goals of the spirit of whoredom is to force mankind to turn their hearts away from God and reject God's purpose and destiny for their lives, thus leading them to destruction and eternal damnation.

Another fact that we must realize is that the scriptures inform us that the Israelites went a whoring from under their God. This indicates to us that Gods chosen people left the safety and refuge of the most High God and forfeited their right to become a chosen generation, a royal priesthood, an holy nation, and a peculiar people. Whenever God's people leave the safety of the secret place they open doors for demonic activity in their lives. The danger in allowing this spirit to operate is that it causes deception and leads people into spiritual idolatry. Spiritual idolatry occurs when Christians forsake the true and living God and worship false gods and practice and operate within their religious system.

I John 4:6 warn us about the spirit of error. It states: "hereby know we the spirit of truth, and the spirit of error."

It's the spirit of error that anoints doctrines of devils, energizes ungodly sexual practices and lust and gives ungodly music its power to transform human minds into instruments for demonic influence. The spirit of error and the spirit of whoredom work in conjunction with one another to bring the souls of men into religious bondage in order for Satan to accomplish his will in the earth. Satan's goal is to use music, sex, and religion to birth his demonic kingdom in the world. Whenever we see these three portals used in a perverted manner, we see the destruction of human life. The scriptures and biblical history proves this point.

Jeremiah 7:30-31 reads "For the children of Judah have done evil in my sight, saith the Lord; they have set their abominations in the house which is called by my name, to pollute it. And they have built the high places of Tophet, which is in the valley of the son of Hinnon, to burn their sons and their daughters in the fire; which I commanded them not, neither came it into my heart."

The word Tophet is Hebrew, which means loathing, abhorrence and vomiting.

This is what a person experienced as he realized what was happening in this place. The valley was located on the southeast section of Jerusalem. It was celebrated as a place of idolatry and worship of Molech. At this place of worship, a large brazen image with a hollow trunk and arms was heated and the children were thrown into the fire as a sacrifice to the idol god Molech. And in order to drown out the cries of the children, the priest would beat drums called Toph or Tophium. Biblical history informs us that as these drums and other musical instruments played loudly as the priest would cut the throats of the children, shedding their blood as part of the celebration. This celebration also consisted of sexual perversions and orgies that were performed among the heathens, honoring their gods. Again we see how Satan uses music, sex, and religion to accomplish his tasks to destroy the human race. The idol god Molech was the main god of the Ammonites. The name Molech means king and the Ammonites viewed this god as the king of all gods. The Israelites worshipped the idol gods of Baal and Molech, along with the heathens. The worship of Molech was celebrated with music, sexual perversion, and orgies. History also revealed that the practice of homosexuality played an important role in this ritualistic form of worship.

As Christians, we have a record that proves that Satan uses ungodly music, perverted sex and a religious system to destroy lives and to eventually destroy nations. The power of music, sex and religion has the potential and capability of diverting the God-ordained destiny of the human race.

> *Psalms 106:35-43 "But were mingled among the heathen and learned their works. And they served their idols; which were a snare unto them. Yea, they sacrificed their sons and daughters unto devils, and shed innocent blood, even the blood of their sons and daughters, whom they sacrificed unto the idols of Canaan; and the land was polluted with blood. Thus were they defiled with their own works, and went a whoring with their own inventions. Therefore was the wrath of the Lord kindled against his people; insomuch that he abhorred his own inheritance. And he gave them into the hand of the heathen, and they that hated them ruled over them. Their enemies also oppressed them and they were brought into subjection under their enemy's hand. Many times did he deliver them; but they provoked*

him with their counsel, and were brought low for their iniquity."

This is a picture of a stubborn and rebellious people who constantly backslid and forsook the ways of God. Whenever God's people begin to listen to ungodly music and participate in fornication it won't be long before they begin to reject God and his commandments.

We see this reality in 2 Kings 17:29-34: Howbeit every nation made gods of their own; and put them in the houses of the high places which the Samaritans had made, every nation in their cities wherein they dwelt. And the men of Babylon made Succoth-Benoth, and the man of Cuth made Nergal, and the man of Hamath made Ashima. And the Avites made Nibhaz and Tartak, and the Sepharvites burnt their children in the fire to Advammelech and Anammelech, the gods of Sepharvaim. So they feared the Lord, and made unto themselves of the lowest of them priest of the high places, which sacrificed for them in the houses of the high places. They feared the Lord and served their own gods, after the manner of the nations whom they carried away from thence. Unto this day they do after the former manners; they fear not the Lord, neither do they after their statutes, or after their ordinances, or after the law and commandment, which the Lord commanded the children of Jacob, whom he names Israel.

The scriptures make it plain that the Israelites and other nations feared God or in other words they were afraid of what he could do to them but this did not keep them from serving other gods nor did it cause them to keep God's law.

7

Let us bring clarity to verse 30 regarding the name Succoth-benoth. The exact meaning of this name is supposed to be booths of the daughters. This was the place where women abandoned themselves to impurities, giving their bodies over to men who devoted themselves to the worship of the Babylonian goddess Zirbanit. Here again we see a close relationship between music, sex, and religion. In many of these ceremonial rights, sex was offered to gods as a sacrifice. We also can see how temple prostitution played an important role in idol worship in a religious system.

Biblical history reveals that male and female prostitution flourished during the time Israel backslid and they began to worship idol gods and participate in their ritualistic ceremonies that mimicked the heathen nations. There was plenty of music, prayers, and dancing at the shrines of these idol gods. According to some ancient historians another group of biblical descendents called the Phoenicians used sex as a sacrificial offering to their god Astarte. Astarte was supposed to have the power to influence nature to produce whatever they wanted. There were times when the women became desperate in their appeal to Astarte to grant them their prayer requests and petitions that many of the women threw themselves down at the feet of Astarte and offered their bodies to men in the presence of Astarte, thinking that this idol god would grant their wishes. Again sex became a sacrificial offering to the gods.

Another form of sexual sin that Israel was attracted to and practiced was that of sodomy. Sodomy is defined as unnatural sexual relationships with the same sex or with beasts. A person who practices this type of perverted sexual behavior is called a sodomite. The word sodomite comes from the Hebrew word "Qadesh" meaning a male devotee to licentious idolatry, practicing sex and prostitution with another man.

> *We see in Isaiah 3:8-9 that sodomy is one of the sins that led to the fall and destruction of Judah. "For Jerusalem is ruined, and Judah is fallen; because their tongue and their doings are against the Lord, to provoke the eyes of his glory. The shew of their continence doth witness against them; and they declare their sin as Sodom, they hide it not. Woe unto their soul for they have rewarded evil unto themselves.*

As we all know, the sin of Sodom was that of homosexuality. Homosexuality was forbade by God and brought the death penalty upon those who practiced it.

> *Leviticus 20:13 reads "If a man also lie with mankind, as he lieth with a woman, both of them have committed an abomination; they shall surely be put to death; their blood shall be upon them."*

Same sex relationships continued to be a practice even during the reign of Josiah while he ruled Judah.

> *2 Kings 23:7 states, "and he brake down the houses of the sodomites, that were by the house of the Lord, where the women wove hangings for the grove."*

Sodomy was practiced near the temple of the Lord and it was the sin of sodomy that God condemned the most. The Sodomites were male prostitutes who offered themselves to other men in worship to heathen gods. In all of these sexual sacrifices offered to idol gods, ungodly music played a vital role in this worship experience. Besides this, there were many women prostitutes, consecrated to idols to attract men into idolatry. The women were prostitutes dedicated to the worship of Asherah. One of the duties of these women was to weave coverings for the gods. The idol god Asherah was one of the main gods worshipped by the Canaanite nations. The worship of Asherah eventually spread to other nations.

Asherah is a Hebrew word meaning "a pillar or image of wood." Biblical history denotes these idols were similar to totem poles and many of these idols were made out of tree trunks carved into certain images. As time progressed, Asherah took on a bodily shape, depicting the male sexual organs. These sexual organs began to become objects of worship and the worshippers started to participate in all forms of sexual perversion, lasciviousness and obscene orgies as a sacrificial offering to Asherah.

Through this practice, we can see and realize that Satan uses ungodly music, unrestrained perverted sex and an organized religious system in order to get some authority within the earth to begin his mission of killing, stealing, and destroying. Whenever we see this type of overall religious system in operation, and if it is allowed to continue, it will ultimately try to take the place of "true" worship.

As stated earlier, ungodly musical worship played an important part in sacrificial offerings and idol worship. Ungodly musical worship can be defined as vocal or instrumental music that has its roots in the fleshly and carnal nature of man. Ungodly musical worship comes out of an un-regenerated spirit that has been tainted by evil spirits and by the works of the flesh. Ungodly musical worship can, however, come out of a regenerated spirit that has been tainted with fleshly desires. All ungodly musical worship is designed to praise and worship idol gods.

An example of how Satan used this type of worship can be found in Daniel 3:7 which reads "therefore at that time when all the people heard the sound of the cornet, flute, harp, sackbut, psaltery, and all kinds of music, all the people, the nations and the languages fell down and worshipped the golden image that Nebuchadnezzar the king had set up."

Again we see how the enemy uses music, sex, and religion to bring people into deception and idolatry.

In actuality, the overall plan of the enemy is to institute satanic worship as the religion of the world. Ungodly worship can bring destruction to a person's life and eventually a nation. Now let us examine this in scripture.

Leviticus 10:1-3 reads "and Nadab and Abihu, the sons of Aaron, took either of them his censor, and put fire therein and put incense thereon, and offered strange fire before the Lord which he commanded them not. And there went out fire from the Lord and devoured them and they died before the Lord. Then Moses said unto Aaron, this is it that the Lord spake saying I will be sanctified in them that come nigh me, and before all the people I will be glorified. An Aaron held his peace."

A close examination of this text reveals that Nadab and Abihu, priest of Jehovah, was found guilty of failing to follow God's methods and instructions on how to properly offer sacrifices to him. According to scripture the priest were mandated by God to use a certain type of incense, they were also told how and when to use it in a sacrificial offering. It appears that these two priests failed to carry out the God-given mandate and instructions of God. Due to their disobedience, their offering was rejected by God and considered as a "strange fire." This term strange fire denotes an offering that is unholy and unknown to God. These two priests violated the office of the priesthood and this violation led to their death. The two priests failed to sanctify themselves before Jehovah and the congregation and also tried to carry out their religious duties while being intoxicated with alcohol. Whenever we allow the spirit of error to control us, and when we refuse to follow the biblical pattern of worship, destruction is inevitable.

By now we should see how music, sex and religion works as a team to assist Satan in trying to under-mind God's plan for procreation and true worship. We need to realize that throughout history, Satan uses music, perverted sex and religion as tools to mislead people in their search for a higher power.

> *Numbers 25:1-3 reveals "and Israel abode in Shittum, and the people began to commit whoredom with the daughters of Moab and they called the people unto the sacrifices of their gods, and the people did eat; and bowed down to their gods. And Israel joined himself to Baalpeor and the anger of the Lord was kindled against Israel"*

Baal was the idol god of Moab and Peor was the name of the place where idols were worshipped. In Canaan, the goddess Baal was recognized as the god of fertility. God became very angry when Israel backslid from him and went into idolatrous practices. Israel backslid from him and went into idolatrous practices. Israel again began to take part in sexual orgies with the prostitutes of Baal who were consecrated to their god to commit such sexual acts in order to seduce and attract men to their religion. It was known that the prostitutes of Moab and Midian were set apart as some of the most beautiful women in the nation. These women led many men into idolatry and fornication. Biblical history also reveals that homosexuality and bestiality was practiced as a form of sacrificial offering to their god. Israel continually failed to remember that God is a jealous God.

Exodus 34:14 reads: "for thou shalt worship no other god; for the Lord, whose name is Jealous, is a jealous God." God warns us in His word about his feelings towards idolatry. Exodus 20:4-5 reads "thou shalt not make unto thee any graven image, or any likeness of any thing that is in heaven above, or that is in the earth beneath, or that is in the water under the earth. Thou shalt not bow down thyself to them, nor serve them: for I the Lord thy God am a Jealous God, visiting the iniquity of the fathers upon the children unto the third and fourth generation of them that hate me."

As Christians in this dispensation of grace, God still will not tolerate rebellion and idolatry of any sort.

Throughout Biblical history we see God constantly pleading with Israel to repent of their whoredom, and in most instances they continued to reject God and his commandments. We need to realize that Satan wont stop his plan of destruction for mankind because he still wants to be like the most high God with the capability of receiving praise and worship from people, as thou he was the creator of the universe.

Satan has devised evil schemes and plans from the beginning of time to try to hinder and stop God's plan for godly procreation. It would be through the avenue of

13

godly procreation that Jesus would enter into the world to accomplish God's will and to destroy the works of the devil. We must realize it is through godly procreation that the seed of righteousness is passed down from generation to generation. The enemy knows and understands that if he can stop the righteous seed of man he could possibly stop mankind from having an opportunity to be conformed to the image of God. If Satan's plan would work, mankind would be trapped in the evil nature of the enemy, and unable to operate in authority and dominion in the earth. The enemy will go to any length to try to shipwreck God's plan for humanity.

In an attempt to wipe out humanity, Satan armed himself with fallen angels in an organized effort to try to stop God's plan, purpose, and destiny he has for mankind. Genesis 6:1-8 gives us some insight into the plan of the enemy.

Genesis 6:1-8 gives us some insight into the plan of the enemy. The scripture states: "And it came to pass when men began to multiply on the face of the earth, and daughters were born unto them, that the sons of God saw the daughters of men that they were fair; and they took them wives of all which they chose. And the Lord said my spirit shall not always strive with man always, for that he also is flesh; yet his days shall be an hundred and twenty years."

There were giants in the earth in those days; and also after that, when the sons of God came in unto the daughters of men, and they bare children to them, the same became mighty men, which were of old, men of renown. And God saw that the wickedness of man was great in the earth, and that every imagination of the thought of his heart was only evil continually. And it repented the Lord that he had made man on the earth; and it grieved him at his heart and the Lord said, I will destroy man whom I have created from the face of the earth; both man, and beast, and the creeping thing; and the fowls of the air; for it repenteth me that I have made them. But Noah found grace in the eyes of the Lord."

God became very angry because the human race cooperated with the plan of Satan to destroy God's plan for mankind. To get a better understanding of what the enemy was trying to do, let us clarify. The sons of God in scripture were the fallen angels that married and had sex with the daughters of men and produced a race of giants in an attempt to corrupt the human race and to stop the pure seed of the woman from coming forth, which would bring righteousness and deliverance to the earth. Satan realized that if Jesus would be born in to the earth He would have the capability of destroying his kingdom and spoil his plans to damn the souls of men. We need to keep in mind that from the beginning of time Satan has made a relentless attempt to annihilate God's plan of salvation for mankind. Scripture informs us that God cursed the enemy for his participation in the fall of Adam and Eve in the Garden of Eden.

In Genesis 3:14-15 reads: "And the Lord God said unto the serpent, because thou hast done this, though art cursed above all cattle, and above every beast of the field; upon thy belly shalt thou go, and dust shall thou eat all the days of thy life. And I will put enmity between thee and the woman, and between thy seed, It shall bruise thy head, and thou shalt bruise his heel."

This scripture lets us know that there are two seeds or two species of people who will constantly be at war with one another, those who have the nature of the devil and those individuals who have the nature of God. What Satan wants to do is to stop the righteous seed from populating the earth that it may not become a threat to his kingdom.

Romans 8:28-29 gives us better insight into God's plan and it reads: "And we know that all things work together for good to them that love God, to them who are the called according to his purpose. For whom he did foreknow, he also did predestinate to be conformed to the image of his Son that he might be the firstborn among many brethren." (KJV). The Amplified Bible reads verse 29 as follows: "For those whom he foreknew – or whom he was aware and loved before hand – He also destined from the beginning (foreordaining them) to be molded into the image of his Son and share inwardly his likeness, that he might become the firstborn among many brethren."

What Satan hates the most is the multiplication process that's connected to Jesus. Pay close attention to the word firstborn. This word in the Greek is prototokos, deriving from the word prototype. A prototype can be defined as the original from which others are copied. Here is the mystery unfolded. What Satan feared the most is that through the life of Jesus, many other brethren would be born again possessing the same potential and ability to destroy his kingdom. Satan's ultimate goal was to destroy the pure seed of woman by which Jesus would come into the world by perverting the sexuality of the human race which in turn could stop the birth of the Messiah and prevent mankind from being born again and keep him from being confirmed to the (image) or godly character and nature of Jesus. Satan realizes that if mankind would walk in their God-given purpose and destiny in the earth, his power and threat to mankind will cease to exist. Satan fears a godly man who will walk in his dominion and authority on earth.

> *Let us look at Jude 6-7 that gives us more insight into Satan's diabolical plan. "And the angels which kept not their first estate, but left their own habitation, he hath reserved in everlasting chains under darkness unto the judgment of the great day. Even as Sodom and Gomorrah, and the cities about them in like manner, giving themselves over to fornication, and going after strange flesh, and set forth for an example, suffering the vengeance of eternal fire."*

The fallen angels, this text discusses were some of the angels that rebelled with Lucifer when he ruled the earth and when he tried to invade heaven and de-throne God (Ezekiel 28:11-17). Jude 6-7 reveals that the angels in like manner after the people of Sodom and Gomorrah and the cities about them, gave themselves over to fornication, an unlawful act of sex and also they went after strange flesh. The Greek word for strange flesh is "hectors" which means another of a different kind. In other words, strange flesh means men with men, woman with woman, and angels with women, all living contrary to their nature. We all know that the sin of Sodom and Gomorrah was that of sodomy and ungodliness. This lets us know that the angels and mankind both broke through the sex boundaries that God had ordained for them. Whenever we reject God and his commandments we will find ourselves breaking through sex boundaries that were established by God to protect one's God given sexual orientation from sexual perversion.

One final point we need to visit is that these fallen angels at one time had the ability to praise and worship God and just because they fell from grace doesn't mean that they lost their inherent ability to worship.

Satan has deceived the world into thinking that by listening to ungodly music and participating in sexual promiscuity and by worshipping idol gods, one can enjoy the best life has to offer. What we all must realize is that history has proven that Satan uses music, sex, and religion to bring chaos and destruction to human life.

Chapter 2

Satan's Musical Kingdom

There is one thing that the Bible makes plain and that is, all Christians are a part of the kingdom of God and they are at war with the kingdom of darkness.

We can see in Ephesians 6: 11-12, and it reads, "For we wrestle not against flesh and blood, but against principalities, against powers, against the rulers of the darkness of this world, against spiritual wickedness in high places."

Colossians 1: 12-13 reveals to us one of the reasons that Satan hates the saints. The scripture states, "Giving thanks unto the father, which hath made us meet to be partakers of the inheritance of the saints in light. Who hath delivered us from the power of

*darkness and hath translated us into the kingdom
of his dear son."*

The scriptures let us know that Satan has a highly
strategic army that moves at his command. These demonic
forces are within the heavenly and earthly realm to assist
Satan in afflicting and tormenting individuals. The demonic
spirits play a very important role in the plan of Satan to
pervert the mindsets and sexuality of singers, musicians,
and other talented individuals involved in the Arts. In order
for Satan to try to overcome the kingdom of God, he must
use tricks and schemes to deceive individuals into thinking
that their God-given musical gift has been given to them by
God to basically please and entertain mankind. The Bible
lets us know that this is a false perception that could lead
many music ministers down the path of lust, greed, and
eventually destruction.

*We can read in Revelation 4:11, and it states, "thou
art worthy O' Lord, to receive glory and honor and
power. For thou hast created all things, and for thy
pleasure they are and were created."*

Most people, in the music industry as a whole, fail to
realize this pertinent fact. Whether they are in secular or
Christian music, the fact still remains that all musical gifts
belong to God and come from his creative ability for his
pleasure.

*We see also in James 1:17, "Every good gift
and every perfect gift is from above, and cometh
down from the Father of Lights, with whom is no
variableness, neither shadow of turning.*

20

The Heavenly Father wants everyone to realize that they have an obligation to use their gifts and talents to glorify and magnify him. If music artists fail to realize this fact, they will become a possible candidate to be recruited into Satan's musical kingdom. The enemy, in his attempt to be like God even tried to tempt Jesus to be a worshipper of him by offering Jesus the kingdoms of this world in which Satan has some power and authority to operate in.

Luke 4:5-8 gives the account. It reads "And the devil, taking him up into a high mountain, shewed unto him all the kingdoms of the world in a moment of time. And the devil said unto him, all this power will I give thee, and the glory of them: For that is delivered unto me: And to whomsoever I will give it. If thou therefore wilt worship me, and shall be thine. And Jesus answered and said unto him, get thee behind me, Satan: For it is written, thou shalt worship the Lord thy God, and him only shalt thou serve."

Satan will use deception and lies to convince people that his kingdom is greater than God's. Satan will use deceptive thoughts to accomplish this task.

Let us read 2 Corinthians 4:3-4, "But if our gospel be hid, it is hid to them that are lost. In whom the god of this world hath blinded the minds of them which believe not, lest the light of the glorious gospel of Christ, who is the image of God, should shine unto them."

Satan's musical kingdom consists of his musical fallen angels and demons that need a human with musical ability in order to glorify their god, Satan. The scriptures let us know that angels had the ability to be musical (Psalms 148:2). We need to keep in mind that Lucifer was the anointed cherub in Heaven that possessed innate musical ability to praise and worship God. We can find nowhere in scripture that once Lucifer and 1/3 of the angels fell from grace, that they lost their musical ability. Once these angelic beings tried to overthrow heaven they were cast out of heaven and into earth. Lucifer became Satan and his angels became fallen angelic spirits. These two spiritual beings work in conjunction with demons to recruit music artists into the kingdom of darkness.

These spirits are intelligent and have the capability to influence the thought processes of people to cause them to make wrong decisions concerning their musical talents and career. Satan in his craving for praise and worship must recruit musical disciples for use in his kingdom so he can continue his quest to be like the most-high God and receive adoration. Satan realizes that in order for him to get worship, he must deceive artists into joining forces with his kingdom. The enemy knows that the average music artist will basically sell their soul for success.

Many artists in their quest for fame and fortune will find themselves in bondage to Satan's musical kingdom and the money and lifestyles that it offers.

> *The Bible tells us in Romans 14:17, "For the kingdom of God is not meat and drink; but righteousness, and peace and joy in the Holy Ghost."*

Now Satan's kingdom is always the opposite of God's so it leaves us to believe that Satan's kingdom is comprised of unrighteousness, chaos and sorrow in an unholy spirit. A good majority of the music in the world takes on the characteristics of Satan's kingdom. Many people fail to realize that much of today's music, such as secular rap, R&B and love songs are birthed out of the kingdoms of this world and the kingdom of darkness. Many musicians and singers cast off their godly morality and take on the morality of Satan's kingdom, which is full of all types of sexual lust and perversions. Christians need to be aware that ungodly music anointed by the enemy can attract evil and demonic spirits that are worship conscience. These spirits are working with Satan to influence the entire music industry.

Whether it is secular or Christian the music industry as a whole does not realize that their music and business practices are being influenced by demonic powers. Demonic spirits have the ability to influence music artists to write music that is demonically inspired. One of the main jobs of these spirits is to poison the world system with the lust and deceit of the enemy.

Music is an avenue that they can use to sow seeds of lust and perversion into the hearts of people. Lustful spirits can inspire songwriters to write music that is full of violence, greed, and passionate lust. Recording artists who sing this type of music have opened themselves up to become vessels used for Satan's purposes.

We have observed many television and news reports of how various music artists find themselves involved with drugs, alcohol, sexual promiscuity, and some even get involved with unholy religious practices. There have been several secular music artists who have been victims of gang related violence. Satan will go to any length to get music artists to sell their souls to him. Satan will offer artists million dollar contracts and sell out concert tours in an attempt to get them to participate with his demonic plan to over throw the music industry. Satan will entice these artists with popularity to the masses just to use their gifts and talents to promote his perverted music and kingdom.

As Christians we need to realize that all music is spiritual in nature. Music is birthed out of basically three kingdoms: the kingdom of heaven, the kingdoms of the world, and the kingdom of darkness. All music that is not birthed out of the kingdom of heaven is worldly and can be demonic in nature. This business about music is very serious. Millions of people are being influenced by ungodly music and messages that come from the kingdoms of this world and the kingdom of darkness. The music industry is a billion dollar industry that has a stronghold on the minds of many. There have been individuals who were inspired to commit suicide and murder due to the lyrics of some songs. Research has proven that teenage pregnancy, fornication, and adultery have increased. Some of the factors for this are centered around pornographic lyrics and images that much of the music in the world is starting to portray. Demonic forces are even influencing record executives and producers to manufacture and sell music that is designed to damn the souls of its listeners.

The reason for all of this deception and destruction can be found in John 10:10, "The thief comes to kill, steal, and to destroy."

Music is one of Satan's main tools he is using in this final hour to bring destruction and chaos on the earth. As born again believers, we need to realize that all music is spiritual and has a purpose and focus. All music has a governing spirit that influences it. Music is either inspired by the Holy Spirit or by a worldly and demonic spirit.

All "worldly" music is not bad, but a great deal of fleshly and demonically inspired music is anointed by Satan to turn people's heart and mind away from God and eventually lead them into open rebellion against God.

As we have previously learned, rebellion is as a sign of witchcraft. Satan is using his knowledge of music to assist artists in making music that is anointed with the spirit of rebellion that will one day lead people into the worship of the anti-christ and beast, which will eventually lead people to hell, if they don't repent. It is imperative that music artists realize what spirit is influencing them to write, produce and compose musical scores. Many artists, operating out of deception, don't realize evil forces are manipulating them. We must constantly be aware that Satan has an agenda. Satan's musical agenda is to build a musical empire on the earth that would promote music that rebels against the kingdom of God and his holy word. One of Satan's objectives is to influence his musical disciples to make music that contains "new-age" philosophy that basically teaches that man is his own god and that man doesn't need to acknowledge Jehovah God as the supreme creator and ruler of the universe.

The enemy's desire is to blind the minds of people by influencing them to listen to musical messages that would cause them to open their minds and hearts to the spirit of the anti-christ. In order for this to occur, Satan must inspire his musical disciples to make music consisting of four characteristic traits that will cause people to turn their hearts away from god and begin to worship Satan.

The first trait is that of stubbornness. Stubbornness is when one becomes unyielding and hard-hearted. Stubbornness is the cousin to rebellion and they both can set up strongholds in the minds of people who listen to music that is unrighteous and anti-christ in nature. Secondly, he uses the trait of rebellion. Rebellion is the act of opposing something or someone. The spirit of rebellion is what empowered Lucifer to try to overthrow heaven. Any persons who allow the spirit of rebellion to influence their life will find themselves out of control and being used by Satan to accomplish his goals. Thirdly, he incites iniquity. Iniquity in the Greek means to bend. It also means gross immorality and wicked sin.

Music that is tainted with iniquity will cause the human mind and spirit to bend or in other words, think and meditate upon those things that are unhealthy and unholy. Music that is vile and fleshly will entice its listeners to experiment with immoral lifestyles.

Now the fourth quality we want to discuss is that of "Idolatry." Idolatry can be defined as the worship of a god other than Jehovah Elohim. The Bible is full of history concerning how Israel forsook Jehovah and went a whoring after false gods. Much of their idolatry led Israel into satanic worship. Likewise, much of today's secular music in tainted with voodoo incantations and spells that summon demon spirits, which will entice its listeners to be lead away from God into witchcraft.

Satan is using these four qualities to enslave the souls of millions of people. The spirit of rebellion is the chief spirit Satan is using to lead people into satanic worship.

I Sam 15: 23 reads, "For rebellion is as the sin of witchcraft and stubbornness is as iniquity and idolatry."

When we study the word "witchcraft," in the Greek it's pronounced "pharmakeia" which means sorcery; dealing with evil spirits and casting spells and charms on one by means of drugs and potions." Witchcraft can also be defined as the use of manipulating powers to control the thoughts and actions of a person. This is why we see a strong relationship between some music artists and some musical scores they make and listen to. Much of this music was written while the artist was under the influence of drugs and an evil spirit.

Research has also proven that there is a strong link between immorality and drug addiction. Many drug addicts participate in sex to help them get money to purchase drugs. Many homosexuals are also involved with drugs as a part of their illicit lifestyles. All of these things are designed by Satan to bring destruction to a person's soul in order that he can receive perverted praise and worship from them.

Sociologist in the secular arena, have proven that music is extremely powerful. First, it communicates an idea or thought and then it influences a view of the thought. Lastly, music has the ability to control and influence our spirit, soul, and body. One goal of the enemy is to amass a musical army of disciples that he will use as his musical evangelist to function as false prophets and musical anti-christ in the world to deceive millions with their deceitful messages.

Satan wants to use his musical evangelists as objects of worship in the world so the followers of these musical evangelist and anti-christ can be seen as devout worshippers of his musical kingdom.

Now lets define the term "musical anti-christ." This person can be defined as a musically inclined individual that is knowingly or unknowingly being used by Satan to make music that contains attributes of stubbornness, rebellion, iniquity, and idolatry. This person is working with Satan and the kingdom of darkness in making music that is anointed to negatively transform a person's mind away from righteousness and wholeness. Anti-christ music can be defined as any style of music that is not in line with Biblical principles of righteousness and holiness. This type of music is blasphemous in nature. We need to realize that all music has an origin, a destiny, and a purpose. Sacred music birthed out of the kingdom of heaven will eventually lead a person into eternal worship with God and the saints. Ungodly music birthed out of the kingdom of darkness will lead a person into eternal damnation with Satan and his demonic forces.

A person will be lead into satanic worship on earth until their death and they will be forever lost and unable to have the privilege to praise and worship Jehovah God. One of the reasons Satan uses the anti-christ spirit in the world is that he is trying to hinder and stop the believers from praising and worshipping God in spirit and in truth. This anti-christ has begun to infiltrate the gospel music industry, causing artists to dilute or weaken the music to a point where the music has lost its focus and anointing. The spirit of the anti-christ is working with singers, musicians, songwriters and producers, inspiring them to make music that will condition their hearts and minds to think and operate in a fleshly manner.

One of the main goals of the spirit of the anti-christ is to provoke people to someday worship the anti-christ and beast. The spirit is also working with the religious systems of the world to promote a one-world religion. This spirit is dangerous and must be exposed to the body of Christ.

I John 4:3 states, "And every spirit that confesseth not that Jesus is come in the flesh is not of God and this is that spirit of the anti-christ whereof ye have heard that it should come and even now already it is in the world."

Satan realizes that if his musical evangelists continue to make anti-christ music and if people continue to listen and meditate on it, that it's just a matter of time before strongholds are set up in the souls of many. Once a stronghold is fortified in the life of an individual they act as an open door to the soul, thus enabling demonic entrance and afflictions, mental distress and even sickness and diseases.

I have addressed the anti-christ spirit in the world today however, we need to be aware that the anti-christ himself will one day come on the scene and play a very important role in religious history. The anti-christ spirit we see operating in the world and in the music ministry and industry is actually setting the stage for the one-world religion and the worship of the anti-christ.

As we begin to look at this mystery person in Revelation, the 13th chapter, we see some important facts about this person. We see that he will receive his power and authority from Satan. This ruler will rule 10 kingdoms within the Middle East. Rev 13:4 informs us that the anti-christ will become an object of worship himself. This ruler will war against the saints and try to overthrow Christ at the Battle of Armageddon. The anti-christ will be a religious leader who will control some of the religious systems of the world. The scriptures let us know that the anti-christ will cause great deception to occur in parts of the world by performing miracles inspired by Satan himself. The scriptures also inform us that the anti-christ will force some people to take the "mark of the beast." We also see in Rev 13:11 that the antichrist will work with a false prophet that will demand the people to worship the image of the beast.

The false prophet is a religious leader that will work with Satan to try to deceive people into thinking that Satan's power and authority is greater than God's. This will be Satan's final and last opportunity to try to be like God, possessing some form of power. The Bible tells us that the anti-christ and false prophet will eventually be overthrown and defeated by Jesus Christ and this will bring complete destruction to Satan's kingdom.

For over 2000 years Satan has been planning to overthrow the kingdom of God and the world in an attempt to set up his kingdom. Satan's musical kingdom plays a part of Satan's plan to regain his position as ruler and chief musical being in the world.

In closing out this chapter, music artists need to be aware of the tricks and schemes of the enemy. Everything that looks and appear that it comes from God may not be from him. The enemy is a master deceiver, waiting to see who will take the bait and become a vital instrument to be used in the kingdom of darkness. Sadly, many music artists are being used by demonic forces and don't even realize it!

Chapter 3

Counterfeit Worship

Now that we have laid a biblical foundation on how Satan uses music, sex, and religion we can go a step further and reveal how he uses these three portals to cause the manifestation of counterfeit worship to become a reality in a person's life and also within the body of Christ. Counterfeit worship can be defined as a fraudulent imitation worship experience that depicts a genuine Christian religious experience that gives the impression or persona that true praise and worship to God has occurred but lacks the power and anointing that comes from having a personal relationship with the Lord. Satan uses counterfeit worship as a mechanism to promote his doctrines of devils and to display his power with the intent of promoting satanic worship. Counterfeit worship is the product of a life that is void of spiritual understanding concerning one's purpose and destiny in God. Counterfeit worship is one of Satan's weapons he uses in these last days to deceive multitudes.

Many churches are experiencing religious phenomenon's such as people speaking in unknown tongues and people being healed by the power of God. In recent years we have seen reports informing us that the statute in the form of and resemblance of the Virgin Mary, has the capability of crying. Some deceptive religious phenomenon, such as the one stated above have their roots in counterfeit worship.

We can see in 2 Tim 3:5 that states "men shall have a form of godliness, but denying the power thereof, from such turn away."

This scripture advises us that there will be religious acts of worship that appear to be real but in actuality a form of deception has occurred.

Now lets examine the word "form" in the above scripture. The Greek word for form is morphosis, which means appearance and semblance. The word "godliness" in the Greek means piety or true-religion. After carefully examining the two words they inform us that a counterfeit form of religious behavior can be found operating in an organized religious system or church that gives the impression that true praise and worship has occurred under the guise of holiness and sanctification.

The roots of counterfeit worship has it's beginning with a rebellious cherubim that became inflamed with pride and jealousy.

In the book of Ezekiel 28:13-19, it reads, "Thou has been in Eden the garden of God: Every precious stone was thy covering the sardis, topaz, and the diamond, the beryl, the onyx, and the jasper, the sapphire, the emerald, and the carbuncle and gold: the workmanship of thy Tabrets and of thy pipes was prepared in thee in the day that thou was created. Thou art the anointed cherub that covereth; and I have set thee so: thou wast upon the holy mountain of God; thou hast walked up and down in the midst of the stones of fire. Thou wast perfect in thy ways from the day that thou wast created, till iniquity was found in thee. By the multitudes of thy merchandise they have filled the midst of thee with violence, and thou hast sinned: therefore I will cast thee as profane out of the mountain of God: and I will destroy thee. O covering cherub from the midst of the stones of fire. Thine heart was lifted up because of thy beauty, thou hast corrupted thy wisdom by reason of thy brightness: I will cast thee to the ground; I will lay thee before kings, that they may behold thee. Thou hast defiled thy sanctuaries by the multitude of thine iniquities, by the iniquity of thy traffick: therefore will I bring forth a fire from the midst of thee, it shall devour thee, and I will bring thee to ashes upon the earth in the sight of all them that behold thee. All they that know thee among the people shall be astonished at thee: thou shalt be a terror, and never shalt thou be anymore."

What we see in these passages of scripture is the account of Lucifer's fall from grace and the beginnings of counterfeit worship. The moment Lucifer began to see himself as a god and began to have desires to see himself worshipped as a divine being, he automatically established himself as an idol god. Lucifer had the great privilege of being a high-ranking cherub that was given dominion by God to rule

33

the earth during the pre-Adamic world. One of Lucifer's responsibilities was to lead people and the angelic host in worship to God. The scriptures already informed us that God created Lucifer with the innate ability and capability to musically worship the creator. This let us know that Lucifer was a musical cherub with the capability of choosing whom he would serve and worship.

> *Now let's read Isaiah 14:12-15, "How art thou fallen from heaven, O Lucifer, son of the morning! How art thou cut down to the ground, which didst weaken the nations! For thou hast said in thine heart, I will ascend into heaven, I will exalt my throne above the stars of God: I will sit also upon the mount of the congregation, in the sides of the north: I will ascend above the heights of the clouds; I will be like the most High. Yet thou shall be brought down to hell, to the sides of the pit."*

What we see in the passages of scripture is that Lucifer weakened the nations over whom he ruled with the intent of persuading his followers to turn away from Jehovah God in their hearts. By doing this Lucifer knew it would be easier to lead them into open rebellion against God. Verse fourteen gives us insight into the reasons for Lucifer's fall, he said, "I will ascend above the heights of the clouds: I will be like the most High."

Now let's examine the events that led to Lucifer's fall. First, we see Lucifer as a high-ranking cherub who once ruled nations and led many people in worship to God on the mount of the congregation, which was an actual mountain where God was worshipped. Secondly, we see this same angelic being with the ability to think, reason and make a conscious decision whom or what he will worship. And lastly, we see this anointed cherub failed to remain in his God created and appointed position as ruler of the earth and chief worship leader. Over a period of time, contemplating on what it would be like to be a God, Lucifer realized that he was created with some God-like characteristics and qualities. Lucifer also realized that he was set apart as the chief musician and worshipper with the inherited musical ability to bring honor and glory to the creator. Lucifer deceived himself into thinking he was divine and that he should replace the creator as God.

Lucifer's statement in Isaiah 14:14, "I will be like the most High" let's us know because of his beauty, position, arrogance and selfish pride, he has the opportunity to be a god.

Lucifer's self-deception led him into thinking that he could become the object of worship within the universe.

When we revisit the scripture in Ezekiel 28:17, it reads that, "thine heart was lifted up because of thy beauty thou hast corrupted thy wisdom by reason of thy brightness."

In other words, because of Lucifer's beauty he acquired from God and due to his body being covered with precious stones, in addition to the splendor of his kingdom and his authority in the earth, he felt he had everything he needed to demand praise and worship from his followers. When we examine the phrase "like the most High", it means that Lucifer compared himself to God with the potential to have faithful worshippers devoted and dedicated to his purpose, plan and destiny for his newly organized kingdom.

We see that Lucifer deceived 1/3 of the angels in heaven to assist him in trying to over throw heaven. Due to this rebellious effort and Lucifer's misguided authority, they were stripped of their God-ordained positions and were cast out of heaven. Here we can see how the enemy can use individuals and angelic beings with musical ability within a godly religious system to accomplish his will.

If Lucifer rebelled against God, he will certainly rebel against the government of the local church in an attempt to get a foothold in the earth and church. We see how Satan's decision to be like the most high, birthed counterfeit worship within the earth. We as Christian leaders and the body of Christ need to keep in mind that Satan's desire to be like God is very alive in his mind and he will go to any lengths to accomplish it. As we enter into a new millennium, Satan is desperate in his efforts to recruit worshippers for his musical kingdom. In his desire to receive the praises of mankind, Satan will use every trick possible to deceive people into thinking that he has ultimate power and authority within the earth.

Let us read a biblical account that reveals Satan's thirst for power and worship.

Matthew 4:8-11 reads, "Again the devil taketh him up into an exceeding high mountain and showeth him all the kingdoms of the world and the glory of them, and saith unto him, all these things will I give thee, if thou wilt fall down and worship me. Then saith, Jesus unto him, get thee hence, Satan: for it is written, thou shalt worship the Lord thy God and him only shalt thou serve. Then the devil leaveth him and behold angels came and ministered unto him."

These passages of scripture reveal how Satan's obsession to be worshipped, led him to tempt the Son of God. We need to keep in mind that Satan needs worship in order to maintain his arrogance and inflated ego. That keeps him wanting to be like the most High. The only way Satan can get energized and continue his quest to be like God is for him to constantly receive perverted praises and counterfeit worship. The Bible lets us know in II Cor 4:4 that Satan is the god of this world and that means he has some authority within the earth to deceive people into thinking that satanic worship is an acceptable religious practice.

We see in Ephesians 2:2, and it reads, "in times past ye walked according to the course of this world, according to the prince of the power of the air, the spirit that now worketh in the children of disobedience;"

This passage of scripture informs us that Satan has access to the heavens. It also means that he has demonic principalities working with him in the earth. When we began to study demonology, we see how demonic spirits can have the power and authority to counterfeit worship or mimic a true genuine Christian religious experience.

I Sam 18:10 reads "And it came to pass on the morrow, that the evil spirit from God, came upon Saul, and he prophesied in the midst of the house and David played with his hand, as at other times: and there was a javelin in Saul's hand."

We should not misunderstand this passage of scripture. It means that God allowed an evil spirit to come upon Saul. And the spirit used its knowledge of religion and spiritual gifts to prophesy or speak a message through Saul. Saul yielded his soul to this spirit and the spirit used his soul as an instrument to manifest its personality.

> *Another example of demons counterfeiting a worship experience can be found in Rev 16:14 and it states, "For they are the spirits of devils, working miracles, which go forth unto the kings of the earth and of the whole world, to gather them to the battle of that great day of God almighty."*

The demonic spirits will begin to operate and manifest themselves in churches as the religious leaders of today fail to discern what spirit is in operation.

> *A strong warning against demonic deception can be found in 2 Cor 11:14-15, "And no marvel; for Satan himself is transformed into an angel of light, Therefore, it is no great thing if his ministers also be transformed as the ministers of righteousness, whose end shall be according to their works."*

Satan will inspire his ministers to imitate Christianity and signs and wonders in the church in order to further promote counterfeit worship to lead people into idolatry.

The enemy has an excellent track record in leading Israel into religious bondage.

> *Lev 17:7 reads, "And they shall no more offer their sacrifices unto devils, after whom they have gone a whoring. This shall be a statute forever unto them throughout their generations."*

The teachings of the scripture plainly reveal that the shedding of blood to devils or any other god worshipped other than Jehovah was a sin carrying the death penalty. Throughout biblical history we can see Satan using man's desire to worship God and using that desire for his own purpose.

> *We can see this in Deuteronomy 32:16-17 "They provoke him to jealousy with strange gods, with abominations provoked they him to anger. They sacrificed unto devils, not to God: to gods whom they knew not, to new gods that come newly up, whom your fathers feared not."*

> *Another passage of scripture we need to look at is I Cor 10:21-22, "Ye cannot drink the cup of the Lord and the cup of devils: ye cannot be partakers of the Lords table and of the table of devils. Do we provoke the Lord to jealousy? Are we stronger than He?"*

Whenever God's people insist on mixing idolatry and satanic worship with Christianity as the Corinthians did, it provokes God to jealousy and it brings about judgment on Christians.

> *We see in Exodus 20:3, "Thou shalt have no other gods before me."*

Jehovah refuses to compete with idol gods that are powerless to bring about godly changes in the lives of people. Satan's use of idol worship and ungodly musical worship is what kept the nation of Israel from coming back to God whole-heartedly. Once the religious spirit comes into agreement with a spirit of deception, counterfeit worship began to flourish and take control of our congregations. The "spirit" of rebellion will continue to deceive multitudes and produce a fraudulent imitation of a genuine Christian experience as long as it is allowed to operate within our churches.

We need to further examine just how demons and fallen angels work together to promote religion and religious experiences within our lives and churches. For clarity in this chapter, we will define religion as any religious experience a person can have that comes from an anti-christ doctrine that promotes the worship of a god that manifest signs and wonders apart from the holy spirit and the gifts of the spirit.

Now let's examine the scriptures. I Tim 4:1 reads, "Now the spirit speaketh expressly that in the latter times some shall depart from the faith giving heed to seducing spirits and doctrines of devils."

Again we see that the purpose of counterfeit worship is to promote satanic worship and eventually cause people to depart from their God. Satan's fallen angels have the ability to reveal false religious beliefs to religious leaders that will teach them and bring many people into religious bondage.

An example of a false teaching is that Jesus Christ was a prophet of God, but he was not the Son of God and Savior of the world. Satan wants the church of God to accept his lies so that his demonic spirits can take full control of our churches and make them a habitation for demonic praise and worship. The question must come to mind how can something of this magnitude happen? We must first realize that Satan's fallen angels and demonic spirits work together to influence the minds of Christians and sinners. The spiritual beings are at war with the saints and have the ability to influence Christianity and the religions of the world by causing people to accept his lies and reject the truth.

I Tim 4:1 tell us that these seducing spirits have the power to deceive. A seducing spirit's role is to cause deception in the minds of people and to lead them astray and draw them into evil works and disobedience. These seductive spirits also have the ability to seduce people into sexual immorality. The second part of the scripture talks about doctrines of devils. A doctrine of the devil can be defined as any belief system that oppose the truth of God. These demonic spirits have the ability to be intelligent and wise and able to function and operate with a level of knowledge.

> *An example of this can be found in Acts 16:16, "And it came to pass, as we went to prayer, a certain damsel possessed with a spirit of divination met us, which brought her masters much gain by soothsaying."*

This is an example of a priestess who was used by a demon spirit to foretell or predict future events. The phrase "spirit of divination" in the Greek can be translated "spirit of python, or Apollo." According to a historical fable, Pytho was a giant serpent that made a speech on Mt. Parnassus who had the ability to predict the future. History states that Apollo slew this serpent. It was believed at this time that if anyone pretended to tell the future they had to be influenced by the spirit of the python.

Here we see how seducing spirits have the ability to impart demonic revelations and partial truths to mankind. Whenever people accept doctrines of devils it leads them away from the truth of God and eventually from holy living.

A good example of the influence and power of a seducing spirit can be found in the changes we see happening within many of our Christian denominations. Some churches have begun to teach that homosexuality is an accepted lifestyle and God is responsible for what a persons sexual "preference" should be.

Some churches are now ordaining homosexuals and lesbians in the ministry. This is an excellent example of how a seducing spirit can influence the doctrinal beliefs of a Christian church. A homosexual spirit is a seducing spirit that promotes a homosexual doctrine and agenda. A doctrine can be considered as an accepted teaching, practice, or religious belief. Another example is that a practicing homosexual can participate in a true-worship experience with God without repenting of ones sinful lifestyle.

Some homosexual political groups are lobbying and are trying to get laws passed that would make it legal to have sex with underage children if it is consensual. The purpose of this seducing homosexual demon is to try to under mind the gospel of Jesus Christ in order to promote the lies of Satan so people can be led into religious and sexual bondage. Whenever the church rejects truth and accepts lies Satan gains an entrance into the lives of many.

Let us keep in mind that one of the roles of these seducing spirits is to counterfeit or imitate a true religious experience that has the ability to fool the elect. Lets continue to examine the scriptures to see how the enemy promotes counterfeit worship within our churches and within a religious environment.

In Rev 16:13-14 it reads, "And I saw three unclean spirits like frogs come out of the mouth of the dragon, and out of the mouth of the beast; and out of the mouth of the false prophet. For they are the spirits of devils; working miracles, which go forth unto the kings of the earth and of the whole world, go gather them to the battle of that great day of God almighty."

These scriptures reveal that demonic spirits have the power to produce miracles that can and will deceive multitudes. In the last days demons will demonstrate supernatural signs and wonders in order to convince people that Satan's power is equal to that of God. Once again we see how demon spirits can mimic a spiritual gift and give an impression that a genuine religious experience has occurred by the spirit of God. This type of counterfeit worship can also give the impression that godly shouting, dancing, and singing has occurred in a congregation when in actuality, a demonic religious spirit is in operation. This type of religious activity is prevalent in church services and gospel concerts where many homosexuals congregate.

This establishes the fact that 2 Tim 3:5 states, "having a form of godliness but denying the power thereof, from such turn away."

This advises us that all forms of godly praise and worship can be mimicked by a person possessed or under the influence of a demonic religious spirit.

When we read Matthew 24:24 it gives further proof of this, it reads, "For there shall arise false Christ and false prophets and shall show great signs and wonders insomuch that if it were possible, they shall deceive the very elect."

Now this term false Christ informs us that there will be imitators of Christ and his works operating with an ungodly anointing. As we approach the close of the church age we will see an increase in counterfeit worship within our churches. Satan needs a religious atmosphere and ungodly worship working together to assist him in gaining a strong hold within the church. Whenever Satan gets a foothold within the church he has an opportunity to set up his kingdom within our congregations.

As I mentioned in the previous chapter, Satan uses music, sex, and religion to try to stop God's plan of salvation and keep mankind from attaining the position of sonship. Satan wants to usurp authority over the church and cause a perverted form of counterfeit worship to flourish so he can continue to receive worship as a god.

Chapter 4

"The Spirit of Homosexuality"

Since we have laid a foundation as to how and why Satan uses music, sex and religion for his advantage, we need to explore how Satan uses the spirit of homosexuality to assist him in gaining control over peoples sexual orientation and sexuality in order that he may pervert their natural sexual drive and cause them to stop the process of procreation thus enabling his seed to gain dominance within the earth. The spirit of homosexuality is one of Satan's most powerful and deadly demons within the kingdom of darkness. These demonic spirits have a documented history of bringing complete destruction and bondage to a person and a nation.

Allen Wicks

This insight again exemplifies how Satan uses these portals to promote the destruction of a generation.

When we research some of the reasons the Roman Empire fell and what role the spirit of homosexuality played in the collapse of that nation, you will have a better understanding of just how devastating this perverted spirit can be. The spirit of homosexuality, a lustful, demonic, spirit has the capability and inherit ability to pervert one's sexuality and cause individuals to lust after people of the same sex. Now before I continue, we need to understand how and where demons originated. Demon spirits had their existence during the pre-Adamic period. According to theologians and scripture, Lucifer was a ruler and had a kingdom on earth and was given authority, by God, to rule over people on the earth. Many Bible scholars believe that these individuals did not possess the capability of being redeemed or saved. When God destroyed the earth, the spirits of these individuals could not be destroyed, rather, they were trapped on the earth. Before these inhabitants died, many of them had practiced immorality and sexual perversion, so that when they did die, their human spirits took on many different natures and characteristics conducive to homosexuality. A homosexual spirit is a disembodied spirit that needs to operate in a human body in order to manifest its personality and sexual behaviors. These unclean spirits seek out individuals in order to carry out their lustful, perverted cravings and immoral acts.

The Bible gives us an explicit example of how an unclean spirit performs and manifests its personality.

Mark 5: 1-5 gives an account of a demon possessed person: "And they came over unto the other side of the sea, into the country of the Gadarenes. And when he was come out of the ship, immediately there met him out of the tomb a man with an unclean spirit, who had his dwelling among the tombs; and no man could bind him, no, not with chains: Because that he had been often bound with fetters and chains, and the chains had been plucked asunder by him in pieces: Neither could any man tame him. And always night and day, he was in the mountains and in the tombs, crying, and cutting himself with stones."

As we study the account of this maniac in the other gospels, it revealed several important facts about this spirit. First the spirit possessed supernatural strength, secondly the spirit caused the man to take off his clothes and walk around naked. Lastly, this unclean spirit caused this man to cut himself with stones.

This picture of the "Madman of Gadarene" presents to us a sadist. A sadist is a person who gets sexual gratification by inflicting pain on others or oneself. This type of activity is called sadomasochism. Sadomasochism is defined as a psychological disorder whereby a person gets sexual pleasure from sexual or physical abuse. There are many people today who practice this type of sexual behavior and who fail to realize that this type of perversion is demonically inspired. Thousands of people have allowed themselves to be afflicted and tormented by this perverted spirit. Demon spirits are behind many psychological sexual dysfunctions and sicknesses.

As we begin to study the spirit of homosexuality, we find that it is an unclean spirit that hates God's plan for procreation and will go to any lengths to fulfill its lustful cravings and purpose. Let us look at just how aggressive and determined this spirit can be.

In Genesis 19: 4-12, we see just how determined this spirit is to get what it craves. It reads as thus "But before they lay down, the men of the city, even the men of Sodom, compassed the house around, both old and young, all the people from every quarter: And they called unto Lot, and said unto him, where are the men which came in to thee this night? Bring them out unto us, <u>that we may know them.</u> And Lot went out at the door unto them, and shut the door after him, and said I pray you, brethren, do not so wickedly. Behold, now, I have two daughters which have not known man; let me, I pray you, bring them out unto you, and do ye to them as is good in your eyes: only unto these men do nothing: for therefore came they under the shadow of my roof. And they said, Stand back. And they said again, This one fellow came in to sojourn, and he will needs be a judge: now will we deal worse with thee, than with them. And they pressed sore upon the man, even Lot, and came near to break the door. But the men put forth their hand, and pulled Lot into the house to them, and shut the door. And they smote the men that were at the door of the house with blindness, both small and great: so that they wearied themselves to find the door. And the men said unto Lot, Has thou here any besides? son in law, and thy sons, and thy daughters; and whatsoever thou hast in the city, bring them out of this place: For we will destroy this place, because the cry of them is waxen great before the face of the Lord; And the Lord hath sent us to destroy it. And Lot went out, and spake unto his sons in law, which married his daughters, and

*said, up, get you out of this place: for the Lord will
destroy this city. But he seemed as one that mocked
unto his sons in law."*

After reading these passages, we see how this spirit
caused men to turn from their natural sex drive to one that
is ungodly and perverted. Whenever mankind turns away
from the true and living God and reject his morals and laws,
it opens a door for immorality.

*Romans 1:24-28 reads "Wherefore God also gave
them up to uncleanness through the lust of their
own hearts, to dishonour their bodies between
themselves. Who changed the truth of God into a
lie, and worshipped and served the creature more
than the creator, who is blessed forever Amen. For
this cause God gave them up unto vile affections:
for even their women did change the natural use
into that which is against nature: and likewise also
the men, leaving the natural use of the woman,
burned in their lust one toward another; men with
men working that which is unseemly, and receiving
in themselves that recompense of their error which
was meet. And even as they did not like to retain
God in their knowledge, God gave them over to a
reprobate mind, to do those things which are not
convenient."*

These passages of scripture inform us that there is a
danger in practicing the works of the flesh and allowing
a homosexual spirit to control one's life. Whenever we
yield to an unclean spirit, it gains a greater stronghold on
its victims.

Since we have discovered how the spirit of homosexuality has the ability to take over cities, we need to realize that Sodom and Gomorrah fell due to immorality. Bible history informs us that the music that came forth out of these cities was perverted. This is an example proving that this perverted spirit perverted the minds and sexuality of entire cities. Homosexual spirits are territorial and seek to dominate and control cities and regions. Wherever we find a large population of homosexuals and lesbians in a concentrated area, history has proven that area is under the control of a demonic spirit or prince and in this case, a spirit of homosexuality.

The city of San Francisco was known as the homosexual capital of the country. A homosexual spirit operates in an atmosphere of tolerance, whether it's in the atmosphere of a city, nightclub, or church. These spirits will manifest themselves in many perverted personalities and characteristics. We can observe in history as well as scripture that practicing sexual immorality opens up the door to other spirits of lust.

According to Athenaeus, the Ephesians were addicted to luxury, effeminacy, and sexual vices. This city had a history of sexual impurity and sexual demonic activity that helped to weaken the moral fiber of that city. As Christians we need to wake up and realize that this spirit is at war with mankind and the church.

Ephesians 6:12 informs us that "we wrestle not against flesh and blood, but against principalities, against powers, against the rulers of the darkness of this world, against spiritual wickedness in high places."

The spirit of homosexuality falls in the category of a ruler of the darkness of this world. These spirits have the capability of possessing a non-Christian and causing mental torment to Christians. These spirits torment a person's mind with ungodly thoughts of sexual perversion in hopes of them opening the doors of their souls to demonic oppression and/ or possession. These spirits attack with a vengeance of evil imaginations and wickedness.

As I mentioned earlier, these spirits are going to and fro throughout the earth, seeking a human body to reincarnate their spiritual nature. A homosexual spirits desire is to hinder Gods plan of procreation and it also hinders mankind from walking in sonship. If one yields to this spirit they cannot be conformed to the image of Christ. Whenever someone knowingly participates in the sin of homosexuality they rebel against their God given destiny and hinder themselves from walking in dominion within the earth. If a Christian practices homosexuality, that person will begin to rebel within against the nature of Christ, thus providing life to the flesh and the carnal man.

As previously stated, a homosexual spirit is a disembodied spirit that has personalities, mindsets, appetites, and ungodly desires. All of these characteristics and traits can be manifested through a human soul that has yielded to this spirit. This spirit has several goals one of which is to re-populate the earth with like spirits so they can continue to lead mankind farther away from his God ordained purpose and destiny. Secondly, these spirits want to stop God's plan of procreation and also keep man from being conformed to the image of Christ.

We see in scripture how Satan used his fallen angels to try to accomplish this task.

Genesis 6:1-4 reads: *"And it came to pass, when men began to multiply on the face of the earth, and daughters were born unto them, that the sons of God saw the daughters of men that they were fair; And they took them wives of all which they chose. And the Lord said, my spirit shall not always strive with man, for that he also is flesh: yet his days shall be a hundred and twenty years. There were giants in the earth in those days; and also after that, when the sons of God came in unto the daughters of men, and they bare children to them, the same became mighty men, which were of old, men of renown. And God saw that the wickedness of man was great in the earth, and that every imagination of the thoughts of his heart was only evil continually."*

These passages of scripture revealed that some of these fallen angels married and had sex with the daughters of men and produced a race of giants in an attempt to destroy the pure Adamic breed. Satan's ultimate goal was to destroy the seed of woman, by which Jesus would enter into the world, so that mankind would never have an opportunity to experience salvation and the redemptive power of Jesus Christ. Satan wanted to utterly stop God's plan of salvation from becoming a reality within the earth.

Let us examine further how Satan tried to use fallen angels to hinder the plan of God.

Jude 6-7 reads: *"And the angels which kept not their first state, but left their own habitation, he hath reserved in everlasting chains under darkness, unto the judgment of the great day. Even as Sodom and Gomorrah; and the cities about them in like*

*manner, giving themselves over to fornication,
and going after strange flesh, and set forth for an
example, suffering the vengeance of eternal fire."*

These passages inform us that these angels did not
remain in their first estate or place of habitation, but left
their dwelling place to enter into the earth to marry the
daughters of men in an attempt to do away with the pure
Adamite stock and thus keeping the "seed of woman" (Gen
3:15) from entering into the world to defeat them.

We must realize and accept the basic truths about the
fallen angels and the inhabitants of Sodom and Gomorrah.
First, these angels and humans had the capability of
committing fornication and they both lived contrary to
their natures or in other words, they lived a perverted life.
This lets us know that they rejected their God-given sexual
orientation and chose to explore other forms of sexuality.
Satan was and is still consistently intent on destroying
God's plan for mankind. Both man and angel broke
through the sexual boundaries God had intended for them.
Secondly, the scripture lets us know that these fallen angels
had given themselves over to all forms of sexual immorality
just like the people of Sodom and Gomorrah and the cities
surrounding them.

The sin of these two cities and the surrounding ones is
that of sodomy. The Bible tells us that these people went
after strange flesh. In other words the people of these cities
wanted to experience the sexual gratification of the same
sex, men with men, women with women. The word of God
informs us to flee fornication and to abstain from the very
presence of evil.

After observing what happened with these fallen angels and humans, we need to realize several things. First, both of these beings rejected their God-given sexual orientation choosing to explore other avenues of sexuality and secondly, Satan used these fallen angels and humans to manifest his perverted sexual orientation. All of this information lets us know that Satan hates God's plan for destiny for the human race. Satan will go to any length to pervert and destroy the mind and sexuality of a person.

We will now explore methods and tactics Satan uses to confuse and pervert the life style of mankind. Satan uses thoughts and thought processes that are demonically designed to attack the reasoning process of man along with the entire soul of man. We must accept the fact that God created male and female with the intention of them being heterosexual. A heterosexual is a male or female whose sexual attractions, both physical and affectionate, are directed to the opposite sex. There is no mention in scripture where God ordained or sanctioned any other form of sexuality between male or female.

It was through the sexual orientation of heterosexuality that God would use for procreation and bring about his purpose, plan and destiny for mankind. Satan realized this plan and had to counterfeit the plan of God by creating other forms of sexuality. One form of demonic sexual orientation created by Satan is that of homosexuality. Satan's creation was designed for the destruction of mankind. Homosexuality can be defined as a lifestyle whereby two people of the same sex are involved in an intimate relationship that involves having sexual intercourse with one another. A homosexual spirit seeks out candidates in order to pervert their minds with the intent on making them sex slaves. It appears that Satan has targeted the church and the music ministry as one of his recruiting places. In order for the spirit of homosexuality to obtain a stronghold on a person's soul it must attack and infiltrate the mind of someone with the concept of an alternative life style. Satan will use his demonic spirits to influence the minds of people to experiment with alternative forms of sex and to accept them as a viable way of life. Whenever this happens it will cause a sexual orientation crisis within that individual. These perverted spirits will attach themselves to the soul and body with the sole purpose of confusing ones mind to the extent that a person is willing to give up their God-given sexuality for one that is rooted in demonic sexuality.

Romans 1:24-28 gives us insight into what happens when a person yields and submits to a spirit of homosexuality. It reads: "Wherefore God also gave them up to uncleanness through the lust of their own hearts, to dishonor their own bodies between themselves: Who changed the truth of God into a lie, and worshipped and served the creature more than the creator who is blessed forever, amen. For this cause God gave them up to vile affections for even their women did change the natural use into that which is against nature. And likewise also the men, leaving the natural use of the woman, burned in their lust one towards another. Men with men working that which is unseemly and receiving in themselves that recompense of their error which was meet. And even as they did not like to retain God, in their knowledge, God gave them over to a reprobate mind to do those things which are not convenient."

Allen Wicks

Focusing on the latter part of verse 27 which states "receiving in themselves that recompense of their error which was meet."

This lets us know that when a person habitually practices this type of sin, the penalty of sin leaves its mark within the life of this individual. When this spirit gains a stronghold in someone's life, that spirit imparts its perverted mind set into that person's soul thus altering that person's sexual orientation, eventually leading that person down the road of sexual immorality and destruction.

The term recompense of their error means that the person received, within themselves, sexual confusion and if not corrected in time, will cause them to wander completely away from their God-given and intended sexual orientation.

Now let us examine some altered sexual identities and see how demons can cause people to reject the word of God as it relate to sexual immorality. These demons also have deceptive powers to cause confusion in the minds of people as it relate to their innate sexual orientation. Many people accept the lies of these spirits and reject their God-given sexual orientation. The first altered sexual identity is that of the bi-sexual. Bisexuality is a perverted orientation, whereby a male or female who's sexual attraction, both physical and affectionate, is directed towards persons of both genders.

Historically bisexuality represents a meditating position between homosexuality and heterosexuality in the traditional American cultural system. Satan uses demonic forces that influence individuals with this mindset or gender confusion. Keep in mind that these demon spirits have sexual desires and appetites that are unholy. Perverted sexual spirits can enter into a person's life by several avenues. One way is the avenue of being passed from generation to generation. Once a sexual spirit gets a stronghold in a person's life, unless that spirit is bound and cast out of that individual's life, it will remain in the lineage until someone overcomes this spirit. Many of these spirits enter into one's life by way of sexual molestation and/or incestuous affairs. Another way of invasion is by participation in sexual orgies with people of various sexual orientations. Sexual orgies played an important role in idol worship in the Old Testament. The door can be opened to these spirits by entertaining sexual fantasies that are immoral. Many of these fantasies can be triggered while listening to sexually explicit music and by watching pornographic movies. Lastly, doorways are opened to unclean spirits by experimenting with homosexuality, bestiality, sadomasochism and necrophilia. These spirits target the souls of man that is the mind, will and emotions of a person. These lustful spirits want to oppress mankind to the point whereby they can possess their spirit, soul and body.

These spirits oppress or possess individuals, and manifest themselves in bizarre lifestyles and alternative sexual orientations. Another perverted lifestyle deriving from these spirits is that of a transvestite. A transvestite is a male or female who wears clothing, usually worn by persons of the opposite sex. Most transvestites are heterosexual, oftentimes married men, who dress in the privacy of their own homes for sexual or psychological gratification. There are also some homosexual men who cross dress in public and this practice is referred to as "going drag" and they are also known as "drag queens." Examples of cross-dressing are males adorning themselves with items or traditional accessories of a woman, such as makeup, hairstyles and jewelry, or females who feel the need to adorn themselves with traditional men's wear. This practice is sometimes referred to as "gender non-conforming behavior." Transvestites should not be confused with female impersonators who are men who earn a living by cross-dressing and performing in nightclubs.

Cross-dressers are said to refuse to conform to their God-given sexual orientation. A cross dresser gets sexual and psychological gratification by dressing in apparel of the opposite sex. Not all homosexual males or lesbians engage in cross-dressing, nor does cross-dressing always dictate one's sexual orientation.

Lastly, let us observe two other sexual identities: transsexual or transgender. The two terms encompass the diversity of gender expressions including drag queens and kings, bi-genders, cross-dressers, transsexuals or transgender. Most of these individuals form their own common ties. They start to identify with a chosen gender identity, usually one that is in conflict with their anatomical gender.

Sometimes transsexuals may choose to live part-time in their self-defined gender, while others may live in it fully. Some transsexual individuals feel they are trapped in the wrong body. This is a deception that evil spirits use to confuse people about their sexual identity. Some of these individuals at times choose to have sexual reassignment surgery with hopes of having their bodies changed to fit their demonic personality. Some receive hormone treatment in an effort to change their gender. This is one of the most vilest character changes that an unclean spirit can inflict upon anyone. There are many Christians and non-Christians alike who are struggling with these perverted sexual orientations, trying to find their "true identity."

It has been noted that many Christian music ministers and religious leaders wrestle with these identity issues and battle with the very spirit that invokes these issues. Satan realizes that if he can pervert the sexuality of mankind, then he can hinder God's plan to have man conformed to the image of Christ.

It is a sad but accurate observation that the church has become the breeding ground for alternative lifestyles and behaviors. Due to a lack of spiritual and psychological understanding on this subject, many pastors have no idea or concept of what the enemy is trying to do in the lives of these individuals nor what seed the enemy is trying to plant in the church. These unclean spirits are waging war against music ministers. Satan is sowing seeds of perversion in their souls and spirits leading to first, oppression and ultimately, possession. Satan wants to pervert their sexual orientation and use their musical gifts in order to render perverted praise through impure vessels.

This too is another example how Satan uses music, sex, and religion in order to destroy moral character in a person's life, thus bringing a curse upon a nation or church. Religious leaders and the body of Christ as a whole need to understand and realize that various evil spirits along with the spirit of homosexuality, is working with Satan to recruit and make disciples for Satan's kingdom. A homosexual spirit seeks to weaken the foundation of the church by deceiving believers into thinking that as long as a homosexual music minister is talented and doing a great job with the choir, then it is ok to allow them to function within the church. We need to realize that a homosexual spirit carries a false perverted, ungodly anointing that causes counterfeit worship and deception to occur within a congregation. A homosexual spirit seeks out a place of worship whereby fellowship of like spirits can occur.

I Cor 10:20 reads: "But I say that the things the Gentiles sacrifice, they sacrifice to devils, and not to God; and I would not that ye should have fellowship with devils."

When a pastor opens the door for fellowship with a homosexual spirit, he is exposing his congregation to a spiritual force that can weaken the foundation of his church, thus bringing a curse upon himself and his congregation.

In the spiritual realm, diverse spirits fellowship one with another. When a homosexual spirit has control of the soul of a person, their fellowship continues in the earthly realm. Spirits have the capability of mobilizing themselves in order to carry out their plans and deeds. Whenever an unclean spirit sees an open door to operate, its goal is to recruit others with like passions and lust to become instruments of wickedness. Demons are activated and seek out people who practice sexual sins of the flesh and the imagination. These demons must have a surrendered will and a human body in order to carry out their sexual cravings and lascivious nature. Any singer or musician involved in the music ministry and submits to a homosexual spirit has opened up their life to a perverted anointing and has given this demon permission to use their musical gifts and abilities to worship Lucifer.

A homosexual spirit is a rebellious, perverted, spirit cloaked with religiosity and has the ability to manifest an ungodly anointing in a religious atmosphere. These spirits have the capability of counterfeiting true worship.

Counterfeit worship gives the impression and appearance that godly shouting, dancing, and singing is occurring within a church, when in actuality, a demonic spirit is in operation. This is why homosexual spirits seek out weak churches and talented music ministers in order to carry out their plan and to make the church a habitation for demonic activity. When a pastor practices homosexuality, he is very tolerant of this behavior and allows homosexuals to congregate in his church and infiltrate the music department, thus making his church a habitation for demonic fellowship and worship.

There are many dangers in allowing a homosexual spirit to operate in the church and influence the music ministry. These demons demand worship out of their victims. Worship entails being in an intimate relationship with God or other gods or spirits. These spirits influence people to participate in acts or fornication. Fornication in the Greek is Pornea and is unlawful sexual acts such as homosexuality, lesbianism, and other sexual perversions. We need to realize that sex is a type of worship and spiritual act that can either glorify God or Satan.

When a music minister is under the influence of this spirit and is using their musical gifts in the church they are releasing an ungodly sexual anointing within the church. Music is a spiritual force, that carries either a godly or an ungodly anointing, that can be released by singing or playing instruments.

This spirit can be deadly because it is the chief influencer of sexual perversion and the strategic demon responsible for the spread of the HIV virus and the disease AIDS among those who are infected through sexual intercourse.

Allen Wicks

As we go further into the 21st century, the church and the gospel music industry is under severe attack by the spirit of homosexuality. There have been countless music artists who have died of AIDS and AIDS related illnesses, in the gospel music industry and the secular music industry.

As religious leaders and Christians it behooves us to remember that the enemy comes but to kill, still, and destroy. The body of Christ must wage war against this spirit that threatens the existence of the human race and has the capability of hindering the flow of the spirit in the church.

As the body of Christ, the word of God warns us about the end result of participating in ungodliness.

I Cor 6:9-10 reads, "Know ye not that the unrighteous shall not inherit the kingdom of God? Be not deceived: neither fornicators, nor idolaters, nor adulterers, nor effeminate, nor abusers of themselves with mankind, nor thieves, nor covetous, nor drunkards, nor revilers, nor extortioners, shall not inherit the kingdom of God."

Chapter 5

The Church And Spiritual Warfare

By now it has been proven and it has been an established fact that Satan and his demonic spirits have used sex, music, and religion as instruments to enslave people and eventually carry out his plan of destruction within the earth. As Christians and soldiers in God's army, we need to understand how the church must equip itself to war against these ungodly perverted spirits that threaten the existence of human life. The church can no longer exist as a passive religious powerless entity within the earth and society. We as Christian leaders and members of the body of Christ must realize that the spirit of homosexuality has the potential to alter God's plan for man's purpose and destiny in the earth. Now, as never before, the church must awake out of its slumber and sleep and put on the whole armor of God and take a stand against the demonic kingdom of sexual perverted spirits that threatens the physical and spiritual existence of mankind.

The spirit of homosexuality and other unclean spirits must be dealt with in the spiritual and earthly realms.

The scripture, in Ephesians 6:12 plainly informs us, "For we wrestle not against flesh and blood, but against principalities, against powers, against rulers of the darkness of this world, against spiritual wickedness in high places."

This passage has informed us that Satan has mobilized a strategic army that has the capability of causing mass destruction in the lives of people and nations. This army has been given delegated authority, by their General, Satan, to steal, kill and destroy at all cost. Satan has equipped his army with the power of deception that can deceive and confuse multitudes. The church of God must awake out of its sleep and realize and recognize that the earth is under attack by demonic terrorist that are terrorizing people, forcing them into idolatry and sexual immorality. The church is under severe attack by the spirit of homosexuality. Countless thousands of Christians and religious leaders are struggling with this spiritual and psychological sin. Many musicians, singers, choir directors, and those involved in the Arts are finding themselves under attack by the spirit of homosexuality that is seducing them into believing that sexual impurity and having an "alternative lifestyle" is alright and is accepted by mankind and tolerated by God.

The church, in this last hour, must rise up and take a stand and take its rightful place of authority and dominion in the earth in order to bring deliverance and healing to the multitudes that are oppressed and possessed by this evil spirit. Satan's unclean spirits are waging war against people to gain control of their soul and sexuality in an attempt to pervert their sexuality, with the hope of stopping God's plan of procreation. These unclean spirits hate the plan of God concerning mankind.

We see in Romans 8:29, "For whom he did foreknow he also did predestinate to be conformed to the image of his son, that he might be the firstborn among many brethren."

This passage reveals several spiritual truths and mysteries that the body of Christ must understand. First, we must keep in mind that God created mankind with the intentions of them being conformed to the image of Jesus.

Now, as we look at the word image, it means in this context, having the same moral nature and character of Jehovah God. When we further examine the word image, it denotes two main ideas, one of representation and secondly, manifestation. Satan realizes that God has equipped the body of Christ with power and authority that can defeat his army and render his demons helpless. What Satan fears the most is the power of multiplication. Each time a person is saved, they take on the nature of Christ Jesus and become equipped with power to destroy the works of the devil.

We, as anointed Christians are the "many brethren" the scripture talks about in Romans 8:29. Satan fears the anointing that is on the lives of believers because he knows that the anointing of God will destroy the yoke of sexual bondage.

Luke 10:19, gives us clarification on the power that is invested in the saints. It states, "Behold I give unto you power to tread on serpents and scorpions and over all the power of the enemy; and nothing shall by any means hurt you."

The enemy realizes the only ones who can manifest a power greater than his is the anointed ones of God that have the ability to hinder and stop his plan of destruction for mankind. The enemy realizes that when the true church of God comes to maturity and reaches its full potential in Christ, that his days are numbered.

We see in Matthew 16:18 and it states, "And I say also unto thee, that thou art Peter, and upon this rock I will build my church and the gates of hell shall not prevail against it."

The word "hell" is defined as a place where demon spirits abide. According to scripture, there are basically five compartments to the underworld. We want to pay close attention to the compartment of hell that is called the abyss or the bottomless pit. This is a region where demons and some fallen angels reside. The abyss is the place where demons will be released onto the earth to assist the enemy in trying to destroy the earth. When the body of Christ realizes that they have the power and authority to bind the forces of hell to keep it from trying to overthrow the church, the church must cast off the cloak of religiosity and take up its sword and begin to wage war against Satan and the spirit of homosexuality.

Countless, thousands of men, women, boys, and girls have been devastated by this spirit. Most of these individuals don't even understand, or perceive what is causing them to think, feel, and act in the sexual manner that they do. The mental wards across this country have seen an increase in people who have mental illnesses associated with sexual orientation identity dysfunctions. Many of these people find themselves committing perverted acts that are un-describable and many have even committed suicide because they have not found a way out of their dilemma and/or alternate lifestyle. We must realize that the average homosexual, bisexual, lesbian, and transgender person feels that God created them the way they are. One of the reasons they feel like this is because they have had sexual feelings for the same sex over a period time.

As Christians, we need to know how demon spirits operate. A homosexual spirit can begin to oppress the thought patterns of an individual at an early age. This spirit causes people to have a sexual attraction and sexual desires for persons of the same gender. Some of these spirits are transferred to a fetus when a female has sex with a male who is involved in homosexual activities. A demonic spirit of homosexuality can impart its thoughts, feelings, and sexual desires into the soul of a person causing them to think the thoughts of the spirit in addition to causing them to experience its lustful emotional appetites. The word of God gives us a solution to help believers war against ungodly sexual appetites.

I Peter 2:11 states, "Dearly beloved, I beseech you as strangers and pilgrims, abstain from fleshly lust, which war against the soul."

As Christians, we must remember that we are at war with the kingdom of darkness. As we begin to take a closer look at how the spirit of homosexuality has taken over and influenced our pulpits and music ministries, we as Christians in the body of Christ must realize that the church is God's mechanism for deliverance in the earth.

Since Jesus Christ is the head and the chief corner stone of the church, we must realize one of the reasons he came to earth.

I John 3:8 states, "For this purpose was the Son of God manifested, that he might destroy the works of the devil."

Since we as Christians are a prototype of Jesus in the earth, this should let us know that we share a common purpose with Jesus and that is to also destroy the works of the devil. The word destroy in the Greek is Luo, which means to undo; loosen; release; set free; or to do away with. In order to destroy the works of the devil, the body of Christ as a whole must realize and believe that any alternate lifestyle outside of heterosexuality is a demonic work of the enemy. The body of Christ can no longer wrestle with the idea or concept that homosexuality and other forms of perverted sexual orientation is one of God. We must agree with the word of God when He informs us that homosexuality and other forms of sexual immorality are sinful and it is an abomination to God.

The scripture in II Cor 7:1 gives us insight on how to overcome these unclean spirits. The word says, "Having therefore these promises, dearly beloved, let us cleanse ourselves from all filthiness of the flesh and spirit, perfecting holiness in the fear of God."

The church must see the sin of homosexuality as a threat to procreation. This spirit has the deceptive ability and capability of seducing individuals, causing them to leave the natural use of their bodies and seek after strange flesh (sexual affairs with individuals of the same sex). Any person who continues to practice this type of sin will eventually fall prey to its bondage and spiritual power, and the need for deliverance will become inevitable.

The church must not tolerate the ordaining of homosexuals and lesbians into the ministry. One of the reasons this should not be tolerated is that it gives Satan an open door into churches with the spirit of homosexuality that has the ability to cause counterfeit worship which in turn, deceives individuals into thinking that God is moving in the church, when in actuality, demonic activity is in control of the church service. Any Christian denomination that ordains gays will begin to see an increase in homosexuals participating in their worship services.

We see in II Tim 3:5, "having a form of godliness buy denying the power thereof, from such turn away."

Whenever we can discern that counterfeit worship is occurring within a church, you must flee for your life because Satan's power has begun to influence that church in a negative way, causing individuals to worship with demon spirits. Any Christian or non-believer who remains in that spiritual atmosphere will become a victim of the kingdom of darkness. The church of God must realize that the enemy has gained a foot hole in the body of Christ. The enemy has dispatched evil spirits to attack religious leaders and influence them into thinking that homosexuality is not a sin. These spirits want to influence holiness in the church so people can began to practice the works of the flesh, which activate demonic activity in the lives of people. The Bible warns the church about apostasy.

> *In I Tim 4:1-3 it reads, "Now the spirit speaketh expressly, that in the latter times some shall depart from the faith giving heed to seducing spirits, and doctrines of devils. Speaking lies in hypocrisy; having their conscience seared with a hot iron; forbidding to marry, and commanding to abstain from meats, which God hath created to be received with thanksgiving of them which believe and know the truth."*

In this final hour of the church many pastors will be deceived into thinking that it's nothing wrong with having homosexuals and lesbians functioning within the music ministry. Many pastors have gone to any lengths to pay and secure a talented musician to bring into their church and to hold a key position in the music ministry. Many of these pastors have willingly and knowingly hired and appointed a known homosexual to be the church's minister of music or choir director. Little did that pastor know, that he had just opened his church up to become a habitation for demonic activity. Whenever a pastor or Christian leader allows this to happen within the church or a religious organization, they have just sacrificed their followers on the alter of Satan, giving demon spirits access to their congregation or followers. There have been many rapes, molestations and sexual affairs that have occurred within the confines of the church. This fact has been proven and exposed in recent months by victims who have been sexually victimized by priest and others involved in ministry. Over the last several years the church has become a breeding ground for homosexuality. In many churches this spirit is dominant and is influencing congregations to experiment and get involved with sexual immorality. This spirit also is influential in leading people into sexual addictions. Believe it or not, many Christians struggle with pornography, phone sex, and many have illicit sexual affairs with members of the same church. We must remember that it is the job of demonic spirits to cause a pastor to lower his standard of holiness and compromise the word of God. Any pastor or religious leader who knowingly appoints a homosexual over the music ministry or any other ministry in the church will be severely judged and disciplined by God.

Jeremiah 23:1-2 is a warning to all pastors and religious leaders. It reads, "Woe be unto the pastors that destroy and scatter the sheep of my pasture! Saith the Lord. Therefore thus saith the Lord God of Israel against the pastors that feed my people: ye have scattered my flock, and driven them away, and have not visited them; behold, I will visit upon you the evil of your doings saith the Lord."

Another important scripture can be found in James 4:17, "Therefore to him that knoweth to do good, and doeth it not, to him it is sin."

God will not tolerate sin of any kind.

Now as we began to equip ourselves to do battle with the spirit of homosexuality, we must understand how this spirit operate in the lives of people and we must know how to bind this spirit and keep it from victimizing others. In order for a demonic spirit to enter into a person's life, there must be a doorway or entrance that gives a spirit the ability to operate. Many people open the door to unclean spirits by exposing themselves to visual or auditory pornography. Any type of pornography can attract unclean sexual spirits.

Whenever people participate in sexual orgies, it opens up the soul for demonic oppression. Any unnatural sexual intercourse promotes and/or denotes demonic activity. Research has proven that many people become involved in a homosexual lifestyle or behavior, as a result of a rape or molestation situation by persons of the same sex.

In many cases in which this has occurred, a spirit of homosexuality was transferred, to the person, by the perpetrator of this act. Another way this spirit attacks people is by way of generational curses. This spirit can be allowed to pass down from generation to generation until it is bound and cast out of a family's lineage.

There are many people who have suffered from some type of sexual brokenness that has opened the door for the spirit of homosexuality. Sexual brokenness can be defined as the inability of a person to maintain their God-given sexual identity and orientation. Some people who have been sexually traumatized, at times find themselves unable to regain sexual wholeness. These individuals feel disconnected from a healthy sexual identity that they once had before they were sexually violated. There are those who have been traumatized due to a divorce or being involved in an unhealthy relationship that find themselves, vulnerable to the spirit of homosexuality. Some begin to experiment with sexual relationships with people of the same sex in an attempt to discover sexual fulfillment. Many males and females alike seek love and affection from those of the same sex due to their lack of experiencing true parental love and affection.

The world is full of people who have suffered trauma by some form of sexual abuse. One of the goals of the spirit of homosexuality is to hinder or stop a person's God-ordained sexual identity and to keep them from experiencing sexual wholeness and godliness. When a person is happy and content with their sexual identity and able to function in their God-given sexual orientation, they are considered sexually whole.

Pastors and Christians must create an atmosphere of love and compassion in the church whereby people who are suffering from sexual brokenness can feel comfortable admitting to someone that they are struggling with sexual issues. One reason the spirit of homosexuality has gained a foot hole in the church is that in many cases victims are trying to deal with this issue alone. Whenever this spirit can operate in an individual's life in secret, it will strengthen its grip on that person's life. In order for deliverance to occur, this spirit must be exposed and dealt with in the proper manner.

The church must be adequately equipped to minister deliverance and healing to people who are in sexual bondage. Let us keep in mind that homosexuality is a work of the flesh that is activated by a demonic spirit. The word of God informs us that the believer has the ability to destroy the works of the enemy.

> Matthew 10:1 reads, "And when he had called unto him his twelve disciples, he gave them power against unclean spirits, to cast them out, and to heal all manner of sickness and all manner of diseases."

> When we read Luke 10: 19-20 it gives us further clarification that Christians have power and authority over the kingdom of darkness. It reads, "Behold, I give unto you power to tread on serpents and scorpions, and over all the power of the

enemy; and nothing shall by any means hurt you.
Notwithstanding in this, rejoice not, that the spirits
are subject unto you; but rather rejoice, because
your names are written in heaven."

There are demon spirits in the earthly and spiritual realm that control and influence perverted sexual behavior within our world system. Many, nightclubs, bars, and pornographic movie theatres, are under the influence of unclean spirits. The church must begin to pray against sexual idolatry because it has become one of the gods of this world system. The only way the church can de-throne this spirit is by praying against the spirit of perversion itself. God has revealed to me that if the spirit of perversion is not dealt with in spiritual warfare, it will continue to afflict and oppress many.

This spirit must be bound and cast out of a person's life, and sexual wholeness and healing must be loosed into that person's life. Whenever we see these spirits in operation in our communities, we need to wage war in the heavens against them and bind their power and authority from having dominion over our cities, nations, and churches.

Matthew 18:18 says, "Verily, I say unto you,
whatsoever ye shall bind on earth shall be bound
in heaven and whatsoever ye shall loose on earth
shall be loosed in heaven."

The body of Christ as a whole must come together and wage war against these spirits with the weapons of the word of God, mixed with fasting and prayer.

Let us look in the word and see how Jesus dealt with an unclean spirit in the Maniac of Gadarenes.

He said in Mark 5:8, "For he said unto him, come out of the man, thou unclean spirit."

We can see that once the spirit was cast out of the man the scripture let us know that the man was clothed, and in his right mind. This let us know that any person who allow an unclean spirit to operate within their spirit, soul and body will eventually have their psychological state of mind altered by the mind set and lustful appetite of an evil spirit. Once this occurs, a person will begin to struggle with their sexual identity and orientation. Once this altered state of mind happen a person will be constantly tormented and oppressed by that spirit. The body of Christ must be aware of the tactics and schemes of demonic spirits. Pastors and Christians must realize that evil spirits cannot be counseled out of the lives of people by using various theories and counseling techniques. I'm not saying that pre-deliverance counseling won't play a role in a person's deliverance and healing.

However, the church must begin to discern this spirit in the church and in the lives of people as soon as possible, before the spirit sets up a stronghold in the life of that person.

There are many pastors and Christians who see this spirit operating in people inside and outside of the church and won't address the issue for fear of being called a gay – basher. Homophobia keeps many people from getting involved in spiritual warfare against this demonic force. One of the reasons the HIV and AIDS epidemic remains a crisis is that the church, overall, has not strategically launched an all out attack on the spirit of homosexuality.

One of the reasons the church is having a difficult time addressing the topic of homosexuality is that many Christian leaders and Christians alike have no understanding on how this spirit and sin operate in the life of a person. No longer can the church remain passive and uneducated about this issue.

Hosea 4:6 let us know that "my people are destroyed for a lack of knowledge."

No longer can the body of Christ operate in ignorance when so many lives and souls are at stake. Churches must begin to equip and train counselors and clergy to effectively minister to those who are struggling with homosexuality, lesbianism and any other sexual orientation and identity.

The church must not reject people who have these sins in their lives, but learn to create an atmosphere in the church that will make them feel loved and accepted. If this occurs, many people will find a sense of security in the church that will assist them in confessing their sins of immorality. One of the weapons that the body of Christ has in its arsenal of weapons is divine love.

We must remember that divine love can fill the void in the life of a person that is seeking comfort and love from others. Many people who struggle with the spirit of homosexuality suffer from a lack of experiencing true Christian love without any sexual favor attached. Demon spirits hate divine love because they know that it was the power of love operating in the life of Jesus that destroyed the plan of Satan to try to keep man from receiving the gift of salvation.

Now unclean spirits operate in the soul realm and deceive people into thinking and believing that sex is love and in order for them to feel loved and accepted they need to have a sexual affair. When the true church of God begins to operate in genuine divine love we will begin to seriously wage war against the enemy. Divine love is one of the fruits of the spirit and it should motivate us to be concerned about someone who is bound by an unclean spirit. When the saints begin to live a life style in walking in love and compassion we wont' allow demonic spirits to torment and afflict others. When compassion is manifested in the life of a person, let's observe in scripture what happens.

> *Matthew 9:35-38 reads, "And Jesus went about all the cities and villages teaching in their synagogues, and preaching the gospel of the kingdom and healing every sickness and disease among the people. But when he saw the multitude, he was moved with compassion on them, because they fainted and were scattered abroad, as sheep having no shepherd. Then saith he unto his disciples, "the harvest truly is plenteous, but the laborers are few. Pray ye therefore the Lord of the harvest, that he will send forth laborers into his harvest."*

These scriptures portray to us the compassion of God in a person's life, one willing to take action against the works of the devil. As we go further into the new millennium, and as we get closer to the end of the dispensation of the church age, unclean spirits will be released from hell to gain a greater strong hold on people.

This is possible only because we are still experiencing a sexual revolution that states we don't have to obey the commandments of God concerning sex and the godly way of experiencing sexual fulfillment. Due to an increased awareness of sex and sexuality in every aspect of human life, many people are finding themselves addicted to sexual vices. Pornography continues to be the driving force that keeps many addicted to all forms of illicit sex. One of the reasons for this is that behind pornography is a demon spirit of perversion that seeks to enslave people in order to live out its sexual desires and imaginations through them.

So many Christians are struggling with issues of sexual immorality and very few people can detect that they are being afflicted. If the rate of sexual addictions continue to rise, many people will find themselves victims of Satan's plan of destruction for their lives. The church must continue to educate the believers on the importance of sexual purity and why Satan wants to use their sexuality in a perverted manner. Whenever we allow works of the flesh, that are sexual in nature, to be manifested, we open doors of demonic oppression and possession in our lives.

Let us look at some of the works of the flesh.

Galatians 5:19 reads, "Now the works of the flesh are manifest which are these: adultery, fornication, uncleanness, lasciviousness."

All of these sexual sins can be used by demons to get a foothold in a person's soul.

Once an unclean spirit sets up a stronghold in a person's life, unless that individual seeks deliverance, that spirit will cause total destruction to a person's mind and sexuality. Leaving them destitute and instruments to be used by Satan's demons. For example, the spirit of homosexuality is the chief influence of perverted sexual behavior and the strategic demon responsible for the spread of the HIV virus and the disease AIDS among those who are sexually active. In most cases, the female is unaware that their partner is having sexual affairs with other men. Satan is using the epidemic of AIDS to accomplish his plan of destruction for mankind. Satan is still trying to stop God's righteous seed from producing righteous off springs that will be a potential threat to his kingdom.

We need to be aware that demon spirits breed filth and germs that lead to venereal diseases. This world is in serious trouble because we continue to reject the word of the Lord concerning sexual purity. If, the plague of AIDS, continue at its current rate of infection, multitudes of people will die prematurely without ever coming into sonship and without ever having the opportunity to be transformed in to the image of Christ.

I John 3:1-3 says, "Behold, what manner of love the father hath bestowed upon us, that we should be called the sons of God; therefore the world knoweth us not, because it knew him not. Beloved, now are we the sons of God, and it doth not yet appear what we shall be; but we know that, when he shall appear, we shall be like him; for we shall see him as he is. And every man that hath this hope in him purifieth himself, even as he is pure."

Satan wants to rob God's people of their divine inheritance that is received by submitting to the transforming power of Christ. God is going to hold the body of Christ partly responsible for the continual devastation of the spirit of homosexuality and the disease of AIDS because he has equipped the church with deliverance and healing power that will set the captives free. The church as a whole has not taken a stand against the spirit of homosexuality because we have compromised our walk with God.

This spirit has been allowed to operate in many of our Christian churches through our singers, musicians, choir directors, and others involved in the Arts. There are even music conferences and workshops where a strong homosexual and lesbian presence dominate the music activities and agendas of these events. One of the reasons this is occurring is because a spirit of tolerance is present in society and in some of our churches. We have come to a point where we have idolized the singing of gospel music without demanding the living of a righteous life. A spirit of idolatry has entered into the church and has blinded the minds of many people. They don't see anything wrong with allowing someone to practice homosexuality and play a vital role in worship.

The body of Christ must put on the whole armor of God and begin to wage war against the kingdom of darkness. The kingdom of darkness has invaded our churches and we are allowing demonic spirits to lead us into idolatrous worship. Whenever a pastor and church allow this spirit to operate in the church, it will summon other like spirits of its kind to seek out weak-minded individuals, who will open the doors of their soul, thus initiating the entertaining of sexual thoughts of immorality.

God is angry with those in the church who fail to open up their spiritual eyes and see what devastation this spirit is causing in the church and in the lives of others. The church must be reminded, that Jesus Christ died for mankind that God's power and authority would be made manifest, by Christians.

Luke 9:1 "then he called his twelve disciples together, and gave them power and authority over all devils, and to cure diseases."

The saints of God must start to bind that spirit of passivity in the church and loose the spirit of spiritual violence and wage war against the kingdom of darkness.

Jesus, in Matthew 11:12, informs us what it will take to win this war, "And from the days of John the Baptist until now, the kingdom of heaven suffereth violence and the violent take it by force."

The church has been given a task and mandate by God to bring deliverance and healing to those who are lost and enslaved by the enemy. We as Christians must realize that we have been given the anointing by Jesus Christ to assist us in bringing freedom and wholeness to the world. When we rediscover why Jesus came into the world, it should motivate us to seek him more for guidance on how to minister to the needs of others. The Lord lets us know the reasons Jesus was anointed by God.

Luke 4:18, gives us tremendous insight. It reads, "The spirit of the Lord is upon me, because he hath anointed me to preach the gospel to the poor; he hath sent me to heal the broken hearted, to preach deliverance to the captives and recovering of sight to the blind, to set at liberty them that are bruised, to preach the acceptable year of the Lord."

If every Christian would begin to incorporate the ministry of Jesus Christ in their lives, we will begin to see the kingdom of darkness take a back seat to the kingdom of God. The kingdom of darkness represents everything that is evil and sinful and that will keep mankind from coming into their original purpose and destiny. As we learn to seek God and walk in kingdom principals, we can learn to live a life of victory and prosperity.

In some Christian circles there has been some misunderstanding as it relate to what is the kingdom of God.

Romans 14:17 gives us an explanation of what the kingdom of God is and what it has to offer everyone who is willing to receive it. It reads, "For the kingdom of God is not meat and drink, but righteousness, and peace, and joy in the Holy Ghost."

The kingdom of God offers everyone an opportunity to come into a right relationship with God and enjoy the peace of God that passeth all understanding.

Lastly, the kingdom of God can give an individual an exciting life full of the joy of the Lord that will ultimately become their strength to live a victorious Christian life.

It is my prayer that the body of Christ will unify itself in spirit and truth and bring total deliverance and healing to those who are experiencing sexual brokenness. The church of Jesus Christ is the only hope for those who have been snared by this vile enemy of the soul that seeks to torment and rape its victims, leaving them spiritually dead, needing a touch from the master's hand.

In closing, I want to leave you with this scripture that has been a source of hope and strength in my life.

This scripture found in Revelation 12:10-11, and it reads, "And I heard a loud voice saying in heaven, now is come salvation, and strength, and the kingdom of our God, and the power of his Christ. For the accuser of our brethren is cast down, which accused them before our God day and night. And they overcame him by the blood of the Lamb, and by the word of their testimony. And they loved not their lives unto the death."

ISAIAH 54:17

No weapon that is formed against thee shall prosper; and every tongue that shall rise against thee in judgment thou shalt condemn; this is the heritage of the servants of the Lord and their righteousness is of me saith the Lord."

Seminars
FROM

Motivation –N- Praise Ministries
Minister Allen Wicks
P.O. Box 2631
East St. Louis, Illinois 62202
Email: AllenWicksMail@AOL.com

Seminar Topics

Minister Wicks has conducted many seminars for churches, conferences, and schools. For more information concerning a seminar at your church, conference, or organization, please contact him at:

Motivation –N- Praise Ministries
Minister Allen Wicks
P.O. Box 2631
East St. Louis, Illinois 62202
Email: AllenWicksMail@AOL.com

1)	God's Plan for Music in the Church
2)	The Christian Musician
3)	Developing a Bible-Based Music Ministry
4)	Sacred Music and the Gifts of the Spirit
5)	The Ministry of the Psalmist
6)	Praise & Worship
7)	Artist Development
8)	Developing a Multi-cultural Music Ministry
9)	The Psychology of Music
10)	The Rap Revolution
11)	The Sacred Love Song
12)	What's Love Got To Do With It
13)	Preparing Your Church's Music Ministry for the 21st Century
14)	Developing a Praise Team Ministry
15)	Satan's Musical Kingdom
16)	The Anointing and Sacred Music
17)	The Art and Craft of Lyrical Song Writing
18)	Race, Music and The Recording Industry
19)	How to Market Your Music Ministry

20)	The Role of Imaging in the Promotion and Advertising of Gospel Music

What Readers

Are Saying

What Readers Are Saying.

This book unlocks priceless information on the subject of homosexuality. It should be placed on the list of "must read" books for everyone practicing homosexuality or have a desire to venture into that realm. If this book is read by every person that is bound by this spirit, not just in the church, but also in the secular world, I believe it will bring about a change in their lifestyles.

Evangelist Bernestine Carter

****

There are realms of the spirit that is not readily understood by many that are in the body of Christ. These dimensions talked about in this book are on three plans, music, sex and religion. This study in MUSIC, SEX & RELIGION probes these realms in profundity. This well researched biblically based reference work explores and answers questions that many ignore or they don't know where or how to begin teaching on these subjects. So don't read this book as a novel, study it with scripture. The more knowledgeable people, the less the enemy will be able to deceive!

Minister Brad Ellis

****

In my 31 years of living I have read many books on different subjects pertaining to Christianity and The Music Industry, but not until now have I read such an excellent, powerful and truthful work of art in literature.

Minister Allen Wicks has displayed such courage by exposing and educating us on a topic (Homosexuality) that has been overlooked far too long in the church and Christian music field. This issue has been a taboo and is finally now being brought to the forefront.

As a professional record executive, singer, songwriter and producer, I truly congratulate you, Minister Allen Wicks, on writing an awesome book that I feel will heal, deliver, educate, and set many individuals of all races in the church community and secular arena around the world free from bondage to begin their true purpose in The Church Ministry and The Music Industry.

CEO/Founder – For Word Records
"The Hypeman of Gospel Music"
Minister Larry Rodgers

Referral and Reference Information on AIDS

1. Christa Ministries/Christa Aids Outreach

A Spirit-filled ministry that provides printed materials including a ministry manual for churches and Love's Shelter, a plan for AIDS support groups.

125 N.E. 185th St.
Seattle, WA 98155
(425)672-4946

2. Exodus International

A ministry of counseling and deliverance.
P.O. Box 7762
Seattle, WA 98177

3. AIDS Support Program Inc.

Provides housing for those diagnosed with AIDS
(405) 525-6277

4. Care-Point Inc.
Provides health care and support services to persons
infected with HIV.
1211 N. Shartel Ave., Suite 802
Oklahoma City, OK
(405) 232-2437

5. Pure Heart Ministries
P.O. Box 1024
St. Louis, Mo. 62276
(636) 679-6815

"About The Author"

Minister Allen Wicks was born and reared in the city of East St. Louis, Illinois where he attended the public school system in East St. Louis. Minister Wicks is a graduate of Southern Illinois University (SIUE) at Edwardsville, IL where he obtained his B.S. in Human Services with a minor in Health Education. While attending SIUE, Minister Wicks served two terms as President and one term as Chaplain of the SIU Gospel Choir. Mr. Wicks also worked with the National Black Choir Workshop and the Gospel Music Workshop of America.

Minister Wicks has been employed with the Illinois Department of Children and Family Services as a Child Welfare Specialist for over ten years. Minister Wicks is a certified and licensed Child Welfare Specialist with the State of Illinois. Minister Wicks has also worked as a Certified Drug Counselor, Certified Drug Prevention Specialist, and a Supervisor. Minister Wicks has also served in the capacity of a Trainer, on various topics surrounding Human Services, for various Social Service Agencies and religious organizations.

For the past Ten years, Minister Wicks has hosted "Lets Talk Music," a bible-based, gospel music talk show that addresses pertinent issues within the Gospel music industry and ministry. This program airs Tuesday nights from 7:00 p.m. to 8:00 p.m. on KSTL 690 (AM), St. Louis, Missouri. Minister Wicks is the founder of "Motivation-N-Praise Ministries," a bible teaching and music ministry that is designed to educate the body of Christ concerning their purpose and destiny in Christ and how God designed us to fill all our roles as instruments of praise and worship within the earth. This ministry is designed to bring deliverance, restoration, and healing to those who are not functioning within their purpose and destiny in Christ.

Minister Wicks is a licensed and ordained minister who has been teaching and preaching the word of God for over 20 years. Minister Wicks is a minister at New Life Christian Church in Florissant, Missouri, where Elder Gary Pleasant is founder and Pastor. Minister Wicks is currently the praise and worship administrator of the church in addition to one of the Adult Sunday School Teachers. Minister Wicks also have a loving and caring family

... And He Continues In The Faith ...

www.ingramcontent.com/pod-product-compliance
Lightning Source LLC
Chambersburg PA
CBHW030341290526
45785CB00004B/1560